W9-ASL-719

Power and Shared Values
in the Corporate Culture

Research for Business Decisions, No. 90

Richard N. Farmer, Series Editor

Professor of International Business
Indiana University

Other Titles in This Series

Power and Shared Values in the Corporate Culture

by
Cathy A. Enz

UMI RESEARCH PRESS
Ann Arbor, Michigan

Produced and distributed by
UMI Research Press
an imprint of
University Microfilms, Inc.
Ann Arbor, Michigan 48106

Library of Congress Cataloging in Publication Data

Enz, Cathy A., 1956-
Power and shared values in the corporate culture.

(Research for business decisions ; no. 90)
A revision of the author's thesis (Ph.D.)—
Ohio State University, 1985.
Bibliography: p.
Includes index.
1. Corporate culture. I. Title. II. Series.
HD58.7.E45 1986 302.3'5   86-4298
ISBN 0-8357-1738-0 (alk. paper)

This book is dedicated to my husband, Jim, who taught me the value of sharing love and life.

Contents

List of Figures

List of Tables

Preface

The vice president of a large insurance company mused, "You can't seem to get the attention of the executive vice presidents unless you value what they value." A cocky young president of a high tech company confides, "The departments who have power here are composed of people who think like me." A graduate students comments, "My cohort gets special attention because we do things that the faculty values in their students." All of these illustrations serve to highlight the pervasive and yet subtle connection between shared values and influence.

Common explanations of why some groups are powerful in organizations usually lead to a discussion of personality factors of individual group members, the authority granted by the organization, or the ability of a group to control important resources. While these explanations are useful and in many instances accurate, they are clearly not exhaustive and may indeed mask a critical determinant. Sharing values with top management is an explanation of power totally neglected in our discussions of organizational power.

In a period of American business malaise, Peters and Waterman (1982), the authors of *In Search of Excellence,* report that excellent companies have clarity of values. They further note that the articulation of these values makes the difference between success and failure. The popularity of this view among business leaders has prompted a spinoff book entitled *A Passion for Excellence* by Peters and Austin (1985). Their book attempts to show through numerous examples why having a strong organizational culture is important.

What these and other current management books are stressing is the critical role that shared values play in the performance of a firm. The term "organizational culture" has become the popular shorthand used to describe the system of shared values and the symbolic representations of shared meanings. The shared values of organizational participants is critical to the prosperity of the corporation, according to the authors of *Corporate Cultures* (Deal & Kennedy 1982). These authors suggest that the rational aspects of organizational functioning are not as important as the shared understandings of employees. A survey of chief executive officers, reported in *Fortune* magazine, revealed that almost all of the 305 executives who responded believe that strong organizational values are important to their firm's success (*Fortune* 1983).

The Importance of Corporate Culture

The recent popularity of the management books mentioned above can be explained in many ways. Perhaps corporate America is looking for the quick fix to their lagging competitive advantage over foreign enterprises. Perhaps, as some suggest, business schools have been preoccupied with teaching analytical tools at the expense of more subtle aspects of running a company. Whatever the reason for the newfound interest in examining the cultures of major firms in the United States, some criticism must be directed at the present approaches for being antidotal and careless in their introduction of the concept of values.

Much of the popular writing on organizational cultures attempts to infuse existing firms with "new and improved" values. Discussions of how to change a culture and develop cultures that are the "best" pervade these organizational self-help approaches (Kilman, Saxton & Serpa 1985). Lest organizational culture become a passing fad—or as one consultant called it "the Hula-Hoop of the 1980s"—closer and more rigorous attention must be given to the role of shared values in the understanding of organizations.

The purpose of this book is to make more precise the concept of shared values, and to then test the relevance of shared values in explaining a pervasive aspect of organizational functioning: power relationships. Rather than suggest that sharing the same organizational values is a panacea for all that ails American business, this book acknowledges the critical role that shared values play in the operation of the firm, and endeavors to explore the nature of values in close detail. A primary catalyst for the writing of this book is my belief that organizational influence is determined by much more than just the control of resources. Time and again my discussions with managers and students have led to a realization that values play a central role in the functioning of organizations.

The cultural components of an organization influence and are influenced by the formal structure of the firm. That is, the shared meanings support the existing organizational design yet may over time provide the impetus for change. Karl Mannheim (1936) suggested that ideological values support the status quo while utopian values criticize the existing order. He argues that the utopian values will supercede ideological values and over time become established as ideological values. Similarly, the shared organizational values will serve to perpetuate existing power structures; but, over time values will change and the nature of power relationships will also change. Of particular interest in this book is the congruity and incongruity of organizational values shared between functional departments and top management in a firm. The sharing of values as a determinant of subunit power is considered in detail.

One unified culture does not exist in any organization. All businesses are filled with subcultures, that is, groups of people who share values that are different from other groups. Given that culture appears to influence behavior, it seems plausible to argue that when the values of a particular group are more congruent with those of top management, the subunit will have influence in the organization. The value sharing between subunits and top management is critical because top managers are regarded as the culture creators. The power of value congruent subunits may be so large as to invalidate or supercede the power a subunit possesses because of its ability to control resources. In other words, a department that is powerless to provide needed resources to assist the organization may be powerful because of organizational values held in common with top management.

The Question of Power

Power is a word that has numerous definitions, yet when you ask an employee which groups have power in the organization he can quickly offer a response. Talking with store managers of a fast food company, I was surprised by the ease with which they identified powerful organizational subunits. Little hesitancy or confusion was indicated by these managers. The message was clear: we may not know exactly how to define power, but we sure know what it is. Equally surprising was the degree to which different employees across the country and in different organizations consistently agreed in their characterization of their own company's powerful and powerless departments. I noticed that departmental power was easy for employees to observe and report on. Finally, I had not anticipated the degree of agreement regarding departmental power expressed by individuals in the same firms.

What determines the distribution of power among various departments within an organization? Two approaches to answering this question have dominated the literature on departmental power. The simple, bureaucratic explanation stresses the influence of functional responsibility and organizational rules in determining power. Newer contingencies models argue that power resides in the subunit that controls resources or critical problems (Pfeffer & Salancik 1974, Hickson et al. 1974). While the bureaucratic explanation deals with functional relationships, the contingencies models stress the imbalances in these relationships.

Over the last ten years the contingencies models of resource dependence and strategic contingencies have dominated research on departmental power. It has been suggested that without the resource dependence and strategic contingencies research there would be no literature on departmental power (Clegg 1975). While the contingencies approaches offer some insight into power, there are facets of departmental power that these models do not address. In particular the models neglect the impact that shared values have on the ebbs and flows of subunit power.

Examining Shared Values

A systematic examination of the relationship between departmental power and shared values was the purpose of the research project that led to the development of this book. The study reported here is the outgrowth of recent writing and speculation concerning the importance of shared values in the functioning of organizational life (Enz 1985a). A cultural model of power is introduced and developed to draw attention to the relationship between power and value sharing. I assert, and later demonstrate empirically, that departments that share similar values with top management will be powerful relative to other departments.

Limitations of the popular contingencies approaches to power are the catalyst for exploration in this book. A critique of the critical contingencies perspectives is outlined and data are presented in an attempt to reconcile the contingencies and cultural approaches to influence. In particular, the empirical findings attempt to test the degree to which value congruity explains subunit power taking into consideration various departments' ability to control critical problem areas. The intent of examining this question is to see if a value approach to power can offer something unique to supplement the existing explanations of why departments have power.

The lack of attention to the role of values in determining power is due, in part, to the unconscious nature of sharing similar knowledge systems or preferences. The organizational values that groups of employees espouse may be completely different from the values they really hold. Similarity of espoused values is compared to similarity of unconscious values to determine which component of shared values is more closely related to power.

Two approaches to examining value congruity, perceived congruity and latent congruity, are presented and compared. Perceived value congruity addresses a consciously constructed notion of similarity between departments and top management, while latent value congruity is an unconscious or calculated indicator of similarity. Both espoused value similarity and the unconsciously shared values will be explored in detail.

The Supporting Research

The data presented here are based on a field study I conducted in two organizations during the period 1984 through 1985 (Enz 1985a). One company, referred to as Food King, is a national fast food chain of restaurants. The second firm, Roboto, is a high technology robotics company. These names are fictitious and some details of the organizations have been changed to protect the identity of the firms.

The organizations studied and reported on in this book were contacted in the spring of 1984. Over a period of seven months I actively interacted with individuals in these firms. Both organizations are small enough that the employees are familiar with top management and the activities within other departments. The study examined all subunits in both companies, including all locations and organizational groupings. A two-stage data collection process of interviews followed by questionnaires was utilized.

The first stage of the project involved structured, open-ended interviews with personnel in each department, all department heads and top managers. The interviews consisted of ten formal questions and seventeen probes, followed by an affect checklist on behavioral dynamics. Interview data were transcribed and coded to determine the frequency of various themes or issues. Information obtained in the interviews was used to develop a measure of organizational values utilized in the second stage of the study.

The second portion of this study involved a direct mailing of a survey to each employee in both organizations. The questionnaire consisted of multiple measures of the relevant variables and provided the quantitative results reported in this book. An instrument was designed and used to measure perceived organizational value congruity.

Limitation and Scope of Reported Data

The importance of values in organizational functioning has been expressed by numerous scholars, yet almost no empirical work has been conducted to confirm the viability of the construct. This study probes organizational values by developing exploratory measures of values and empirically testing the relationship of value congruity to departmental power. Three limitations of the present study are noteworthy.

First, the unit of analysis in this study was an easily identifiable unit—the department. Although evidence is presented to suggest that the department is a meaningful unit of analysis, it is plausible that other subdivisions could capture value similarity in a more exact or significant way. The structurally determined subunit may not be the culturally defined subunit. A second limitation is the exclusion of contextual factors as possible moderators of the relationships. The nature of the industry, a firm's stage in its life cycle, or shifts in the environment may all weaken or invalidate the influence of values. Finally, the cross-sectional nature of the study makes it impossible to make causal statements concerning the relationship between value congruity and power or to observe the process of change.

The limitations mentioned involve issues that can be resolved through future research into the role of value congruity. The question of whether value congruity is functional or dysfunctional for the organization was not addressed. The nature of departmental motives for expressed value similarity with top management also poses an interesting area for further investigation. Future research should be directed toward refining measures of organizational values and value congruity.

Overview of Chapters

The remainder of this book is divided into six chapters. The first chapter provides a clarification and review of the literature on organizational power. Two popular approaches to explaining power are discussed. The chapter concludes with the presentation of a third, cultural approach to studying power. This approach to organizational power is developed in order to clarify the linkage between power and shared values.

To understand the role that organizational values play in explaining power, chapter 2 provides a description of values and why top management is essential to our understanding of power. Based on 81 interviews with employees in the two organizations, specific values are discussed in chapter 2. Values considered both important and unimportant to organizational functioning are discussed.

In the third chapter the issue of value sharing is considered. Two forms of value similarity are presented in this chapter: values that are espoused or expressed and values that top management and different groups of employees unconsciously share (latent values). A newly developed measure of organizational value similarity is presented in this chapter.

Chapter 4 presents empirical support for the connection between sharing values and departmental power. The views of top management and all departmental employees are examined to provide multiple perspectives on values and power.

A case history of a small enterprise is presented in chapter 5. This illustration shows how a growing T-shirt company relies almost exclusively on shared values to determine departmental influence.

The final chapter summarizes the implications for studying

organizational values. The process of institutionalizing values is discussed in detail. The chapter concludes with a discussion of both the impact of shared values on organizational functioning and possible areas for future study.

Five appendices are included at the end of the book to provide detailed information for the interested reader. A description of the methodology employed in the study is provided in appendix A and a detailed explanation of each measure used in the study is presented. Appendix B includes the interview guide used in the study. Appendix C provides the instrument developed to measure perceived value congruity. Listed in appendix D are the research hypotheses that guided the study. Finally, detailed summary statistics corresponding to each of the hypotheses are tabled in appendix E.

Final Note

I would be remiss if I did not take an opportunity to express my sincere appreciation to several persons who were instrumental in making this book a reality. First, I owe a great debt to Dr. James McFillen, my graduate advisor at Ohio State University. Our consulting partnership allowed me the opportunity to observe the role of value sharing firsthand. Dr. H. Randolph Bobbitt, Jr. of O.S.U. also deserves thanks for his support during the data collection stage upon which this book is based.

My move to Indiana University after graduate school has afforded me the pleasure of contact with several stimulating scholars. In particular, I wish to acknowledge the insightful comments of Dr. Andrew Weiss on portions of the first chapter. To my colleagues in the management department I express appreciation for their support and encouragement. A sincere thank you must also go to Mary Post who willingly edited this book and deserves a great deal of the credit for improving the final draft. To my parents I am profoundly grateful for constant and enduring support. Finally, a special thanks goes to my husband, James C. McKee, who endured my long work hours and was always there during the little crises.

Cathy A. Enz
Bloomington, Indiana
December 1985

1

Determining Power in Organizations

Organizations are filled with powerful people and groups. In the last ten years observers and participants in organizations have become increasingly interested in learning how power works. The fascination with acquiring and using power is illustrated in the numerous trade books on the subject. Because the concept of power is generally considered to be elusive, intangible and ubiquitous our understanding of power in organizations has been limited. Cartwright (1965, 3) has pointed out that the literature is "scattered, homogeneous and even chaotic." In spite of its conceptual and empirical problems, however, the concept continues to be of interest.

Power is a compelling topic because it refers to a phenomenon we experience at various levels and in numerous ways. As Bertrand Russell noted, "The fundamental concept in social science is power, in the same sense in which energy is the fundamental concept in physics" (1938, 12). But even if we agree that power is pervasive in organizations we cannot agree on what determines who has power. It is insufficient merely to examine who has power without asking what mechanisms provide the context for the acquisition and use of power.

An important distinction must be drawn at the onset between individual power that focuses on personal influence, and organizational power that centers on organizationally relevant activities and operations. Individual power is held by people who use it for their own personal ends. Organizational power is held by a subunit and is used for organizational ends. Organizational power, as examined at the subunit level, addresses directly the functioning of the organization while individual power often only marginally impacts on organizational functioning. Individual power specifically addresses interpersonal behaviors, but subunit power helps to explain how the organization operates.

Typically, power at the departmental level is explained by the structuring of functional areas or by subunit control of critical unknowns. Much has been written on the formal mechanisms (structures) that facilitate the acquisition of power and power obtained because subunits control environmental uncertainties. As yet, little research has attempted to directly investigate the impact of shared organizational values on the process of obtaining departmental power.

This chapter lays a theoretical foundation for the examination of values in the context of organizational power. Before developing a model of the relationship between value congruity and power, the existing literature on power will be reviewed. In particular the well known critical contingencies explanations of power will be presented and critiqued. The chapter will conclude with the presentation of a value congruity model of departmental power.

Perspectives on Power

Many researchers in the behavioral sciences have focused on individual power. For example, Kipnis (1976) has examined the powerholder, Mechanic (1962) has explored the powerless, and French and Raven (1959) have investigated sources of power. Examining the power of an individual and answering the question "why" has consumed a great deal of attention. People who have power want to keep it, those who don't have it want it, and most of us want to reduce the power of others over us.

Emerson (1962) provides an alternative to the psychological treatment of power. He argues for viewing power as a facet of the social setting, not as an attribute of individuals. By examining the power of groups, influence can be understood as a determinant of organizational actions rather than as a characteristic of the person. Emphasis at the individual level is on determining the tactics or foundations upon which people work the system. Examining power at the departmental level stresses determining why some subunits are more capable of affecting the actions of the firm.

Power at the group level is most frequently observed in two ways: hierarchically (vertically) or laterally (horizontally). These orientations, while different, are both linked to the organizational structure (i.e. the division of labor and chain of command). Vertical power is closely linked to the authority system of the firm, while lateral power is relevant in ambiguous situations where clearly defined responsibility is not evident.

Vertical power is an orientation toward power that is based on position in the organizational hierarchy. Tannenbaum and Kahn (1958) were pioneers in conducting research on the differences in power of groups at different levels in the hierarchy. Their work stressed the distribution of power within organizations through the use of diagrams called control graphs. These researchers endeavored to examine power differences by position and degree while offering some insightful determinants and consequences of power (Tannenbaum 1968).

Typically, the examination of vertical power suggests that powerful groups are those at higher levels in the organization structure. An organization imbues some levels with a greater ability to specify commands that are obeyed by a given group of persons. Power that is granted by virtue of position is frequently called authority. Those at higher levels in the organization's hierarchy have more power to influence others than those lower in the organization. At the very top of the organization are the owners or leaders who ultimately dictate the philosophies and strategies of the firm. Because this group of leaders cannot be everywhere, they delegate to those below them the authority to act as agents of the firm.

Lateral power stresses power that different groups at the same level in the organization have over each other. This type of power is referred to as lateral because the parties involved are equal in the organizational hierarchy. An example of lateral power is the influence that the accounting department has over the marketing department in an organization. Perrow's (1970, 59) warning that we are preoccupied with individual power and have neglected the department provided significant impetus for many to ask the question, "Why do different subunits have different levels of influence?"

In this book, the focus is on lateral power. I will attempt to answer Perrow's question by examining lateral power among departments in two companies. The department was chosen as the unit of analysis for three reasons. First, internal interest groups form in organizations, and a natural grouping is around functional expertise. Power struggles among departments are well documented in the organizational literature. Second, by examining departmental power we eliminate power due to level in the hierarchy (vertical power) or the personal influence of specific personnel. Finally, the department is a distinct subunit to which employees identify. Hence, the department constitutes a meaningful unit of analysis.

Power Defined

What is power? People seem to know power when they see it, but attempts at providing a generally acceptable definition are fraught with inconsistency at best and contradiction at worst. The variety of meanings is due in part to the everyday use of the term. Schopler (1965) observed that the numerous connotative and denotative meanings of the term make theory development difficult. Obviously the frequent and casual use of the term makes the task of the theorist difficult. Thus, to use power systematically and precisely requires some attention to definition.

Table 1-1 provides a brief list of commonly used definitions of power. The list of definitions is divided into two categories, those dealing with power as an individual phenomena (interpersonal level) and those defining power as

Table 1-1.   Common Definitions of Power.

Social Unit Definitions of Power

"Power we may define as the realistic capacity of a system-unit to actualize its interests within the context of system-interaction and in this sense exert influence on processes in the system."
(Parsons 1960, 221)

"The ability of those who possess power to bring about the outcomes they desire."
(Salancik & Pfeffer 1974, 3)

"... it [power] marks the ability of one person or group of persons to influence the behavior of others, that is, to change the probabilities that others will respond in certain ways to specified stimuli."
(Kaplan 1950, 12)

"Power may be defined as the production of intended effects."
(Russell 1938, 35)

Interpersonal Definitions of Power

"Power is the probability that one actor within a social relationship will be in a position to carry out his own will despite resistance, regardless of the basis on which this probability rests."
(Weber 1947, 152)

"Power is the ability of persons as groups to impose their will on others despite resistance...."
(Blau 1964, 115)

"A has power over B to the extent that he can get B to do something that B would not otherwise do."
(Dahl 1957, 202–3)

"Power is the capacity of some persons to produce intended and foreseen effects on others."
(Wrong 1979, 2)

"Person A could cause person B to do something which was contrary to B's desire."
(French & Raven 1959, 152)

---

a product of the social setting (social-unit level). The unit of analysis is only one of several ways definitions differ. Some authors distinguish between the terms force, influence, control, authority, dominance, persuasion and power; other authors use the term power as all inclusive. Power to some is asymmetric; that is, power flows in one direction from a powerful group to a powerless group. Other conceptions of power allow for symmetrical or reciprocal influence among different groups.

The generality of power raises another definitional distinction. Power has been conceptualized as a general phenomenon observable in numerous contexts and also as situation specific. Treating power as legitimate versus illegitimate is another fundamental distinction between different types of power research. Finally, power has been viewed as either a zero-sum concept where the possession by one group precludes the possession by another, or as a sharable commodity where two groups can both possess power.

Clearly any study of power must be limited in its focus and rely on some definitional assumptions. Here, I have limited investigation to an examination of power at the departmental level, where power is regarded as a facet of social organizing. Further, power is distinguished from force, dominance and authority. This assumption is made because force and dominance imply coercive components of power. Wrong (1979) has captured force as restricting freedom and has associated the term with threats and ultimately violence. Clearly the focus here is on organizational activities where the intent of power is not to inflict physical or mental harm. In addition, authority addresses the legitimate use of power or power that is stable and institutionalized. The concept of authority suggests that powerholders have a right to influence and a legitimate ability to compel obedience. By examining subunit power, we are interested in influence that deviates from the structural or legitimate uses of power, and is thus political in nature.

Political power suggests the use of power in situations where clear rules and responsibilities do not exist. This subcategory of power is regarded as situational, but is grounded in an organizational history that allows for the overlap of power attempts in unique contexts. Hence, the power of a subunit may be determined in one context and then generalized to similar but not identical situations. Political power operates in the context of dissent, ambiguity, and instability, but is not completely defined by current situations.

A final assumption regarding power that is made here is the symmetrical nature of departmental influence. This assumption suggests that two different groups may influence each other. Power flows back and forth among subunits and no single department controls all of the political power all of the time.

One critical conceptual issue also emerges from the definitional controversy. Should actual and potential power be distinguished and/or isolated for purposes of theorizing and analysis? Potential power suggests that power does not have to be exercised to exist. Actual power is power that is enacted or observed. Consideration of power as potential is in agreement with many early theorists' conceptualizations (Cartwright 1965, March 1955). These theorists suggest that power is the potential to act without requiring actual exercise. Others advocate a behavioral view of power that depends on observable (actual) behaviors (Dahl 1957). Treating power as exclusively potential or actual power possesses an important theoretical question.

Wrong's (1968, 1979) solution to the problem of segmenting and focusing on one or the other aspects of power is to combine both potential and actual power into a concept he refers to as capacity. Defining power as capacity allows for a department to "have" power without exercising it, so long as it is believed that the department will exercise it. Capacity is not identical to potential because it relies on the relationship between actors, based in part on previous actions. Hence, capacity is the ability to affect others.

Has influence taken place only when some demonstration of power occurs? Does a department have power if it does not exercise that power? By only considering power in situations when actions occur, instances when a department chooses not to use power are excluded. By examining potential power only, the researcher is forced to rely exclusively on attributions or perceptions. By combining potential and actual, as Wrong does, the theorist is in a position to combine the strength of power attributions with a history of actions. It seems plausible to assert that departments can have power without exercising it. But power is also a relationship between departments based on a history of actions.

Following the work of Wrong (1979), power will be treated as both the potential for power and actual power. This orientation suggests that a department may have power without actually exercising it, assuming that potential power is confirmed by actions or agreement from parties involved in interaction. Power will be defined here as the capacity of a department to affect various issues within the organizational context and in doing so to exert influence on organizational activities and direction. Defining power in this way better captures the interaction of actual and potential power.

Approaches to Power

A rational approach to the study of power is evidenced by examining hierarchical authority. Weber's (1978) understanding of rational legal domination [translated from the German as "authority"] provides the theoretical foundation for this structural explanation of power. Authority rests on the rules and rights of those in legitimate positions of leadership. Using a rational model, authority is determined by functional responsibility and organizational rules. The distribution of power is based on the division of labor, suggesting that different functional departments will have authority over the areas of their competency. Finally, power under a rational model is stable and impersonal. Thus, power is based on legitimate claims or rights inherent in positions rather than in people. For example, an accounting department's control over the financial aspects of an organization is legitimate because it is functionally rational. To avoid the ambiguity which may arise concerning accounting issues, this department is responsible for establishing procedures and guidelines to inform decisions of a financial nature.

However, Weber's perspective fails to account for what seems obvious to the casual observer of organizations: informal influence is present beyond functionally rational authority. Informal influence processes and irrational aspects of power have led many to political explanations of why some groups have more power than others. Outsiders and newcomers may look on with amazement when they see subunits influence organizational decisions outside of their functional areas of expertise. Why do these groups have power beyond that granted by functional legitimacy? Attempts to understand seemingly irrational power relationships have prompted examinations of a more political nature.

The dominant political approaches to explaining intraorganizational power are the critical contingencies theories (Pfeffer & Salancik 1974, Hickson et al. 1974). The critical contingencies theories rely on a situational (contingencies) model to explain power. For these theorists, the groups that are most capable of controlling critical problem areas possess power. This explanation suggests that power relationships are unstable and change with the ability of a subunit to control the critical problem. Most critical problems are determined by factors in the environment, according to this view; thus, external factors determine in large measure what is critical. For example, in the event of a lawsuit, the legal department is most capable of handling the problem and thus has power to influence decisions. Proponents of the critical contingencies theories would suggest that the legal department will gain power that will carry over into other situations. Another example presented in the literature (Pfeffer & Salancik 1974) was the influence which some departments in a large university possessed because these departments were better able to obtain contract and grant monies and these resources were regarded as invaluable to the organization. Thus the contingencies approach argues that power is granted to departments that are able to control or manage important environmental uncertainties.

The last approach to the study of power, and the one this book examines in detail, will be called a cultural model of power. Using this orientation, departmental consensus with top management on important organizational values determines which subunits possess political power. The distribution of power is grounded in value congruity and is stable over time, though not as stable as formal authority. This approach suggests that the groups with the greatest influence are those with organizational values that are congruent with the leaders' values. A cultural model is similar to the contingencies model in that both are most appropriate in situations where organizationally relevant decisions are made that are not defined by or do not fit into the formal authority structure (Enz 1985a; Weiss & Enz 1985). In situations characterized by dissent, ambiguity and instability, the department that can claim values that are congruent with those of the leadership will possess power.

An example used by Weiss and Enz (1985) serves to illustrate the role of values in determining power. Assume that inventory stockouts are a source of ambiguity and general dissent between departments. To those in the purchasing department, stockouts are a necessary event in order to minimize the number of days of inventory on hand. In contrast, the marketing personnel view stockouts as a customer service problem posing a threat to both present and future sales. If purchasing has its way, inventory will remain low; if marketing has its way, inventory will increase. Which department will successfully exert influence in this situation? Two different preference states exist for resolving the problem, one favoring cost minimization and the other stressing customer service. According to the cultural model, the department that successfully exerts influence will be the department whose organizational values (preference states) are most closely aligned with those of top management. If the leadership of the company values customer service above all else, marketing will be more powerful in this and future situations where the conflicting value preferences arise. This suggests that power that is determined by shared values can become stable and ultimately can be institutionalized as a formal function of the organization.

Three distinct approaches to power have been presented: the rational, contingencies, and cultural models. Table 1-2 summarizes these approaches as they apply to intraorganizational power. The assumptions regarding the determinants, distribution, and stability of power are highlighted in the table. The purpose of this summary is to illustrate the distinct orientations of various models of power.

A decade ago researchers demonstrated that a rational model of power was inadequate to explain how organizations really function. These researchers introduced a contingencies model as an alternative. It is the objective of this book to demonstrate that a contingencies model is not totally sufficient either. The rational model is grounded in a conception of power as authority, while the contingencies and cultural models examine political features of power. Greater attention will be placed on examining the political models and later linking the political with the rational model to provide an overall picture of organizational power.

Clearly each model provides useful information. It is hoped that by developing a cultural model of power in the chapters to follow and presenting evidence to support this model, the political models of contingencies theorists will be supplemented and in some ways challenged. In addition, the development of a cultural model allows an opportunity to fit the contingencies and rational approaches to power into a framework that will shed light on the process of determining departmental power. Before an exploration of the cultural model is appropriate, the contingencies theories deserve further examination.

Table 1-2.   Approaches to Departmental Power.

	Rational Model	Contingencies Model	Cultural Model
Determinants of Departmental Power	Functional responsibility & organizational rules.	Control of critical problems or uncertainties.	Consensus with top management on important organizational values.
Distribution of Power	Based on division of labor and authority.	Based on the ability to control critical problems.	Based on whether a department is value congruent with top mgt.
Stability of Power	Stable and impersonal.	Unstable Changes with the ability of a subunit to control critical problems.	Stable, but capable of adjusting. Values are enduring, but capable of change.

Controlling Contingencies: An Explanation of Power

Critical contingencies is an all inclusive term used to express both the resource dependence and strategic contingencies perspectives. The strategic contingencies (Hickson et al. 1971) and resource dependence (Salancik & Pfeffer 1974) models are similar in that they focus on structural explanations of power. They argue that the power of a department is determined by the situational importance of its functions, tasks, or activities (Pfeffer 1981b). Power comes from having control over critical resources that other departments need. The difference between these two perspectives lies in the variables they specify as being critical in determining power. For a strategic contingencies perspective the critical variables are coping with uncertainty, substitutability of activities and centrality of activities. In a resource dependence perspective, the critical variable is control of scarce and valued resources.

Figure 1-1 presents a model of power based on the work of Pfeffer (1981b) and includes the strategic contingencies model. The model suggests that the environment determines which departments are best suited to provide critical resources or solve critical problems. Department power is determined by a subunit's ability to respond to the environment. Once the department has acquired power, it will employ this power in new situations and will over time increase its formal authority.

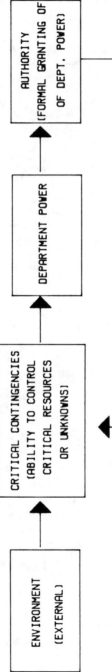

Figure 1-1. A Critical Contingencies Model of Power.

Implicit in the model of power (see figure 1-1) is the logic that unstable situations necessitate political action by departments most able to cope with the unknown. Somewhat inconsistently, the critical contingencies theorists also indicate that the actions of the now powerful department are codified (institutionalized) and thus reinforce the perpetuation of a particular department's power. The unanswered question in this perspective is: now that a stable state exists, what is necessary for departmental power to vary again? If another change in environmental threats will change the power structure again, the model is painfully unstable. Clearly some necessary components of power relationships and their functioning over time are absent from this model and these factors will be explored in detail later in this chapter.

Both a strategic contingencies and resource dependence approach to intraorganizational power have dominated the research on departmental power. Clegg (1975) argues that without these two orientations there would be no research on intraorganizational power. Even with the presence of these models, little empirical work has been conducted. These perspectives have been embraced by many and used as a foundation for the exploration of organizational and interorganizational issues significantly unrelated to power. Hence, critical contingencies models are the dominant political explanations of power, but little verification and extension actually exists.

Strategic Contingencies

The strategic contingencies perspective on power has its foundation in the work of Crozier (1964) and Cyert and March (1963). The theory is based on, but departs from, the rational model which views the organization as an open system that faces many environmental uncertainties. Owners and founders of organizations design their firms to cope with the uncertainties. One aspect of designing is the division of labor by subunits, each responsible for controlling a particular function. Where strategic contingencies departs from the rational model is in its attempt to explain political power or influence outside of the rational authority structure. Because subunits are highly dependent on each other, those subunits capable of providing others with needed, critical, and scarce resources will gain power.

Hickson et al. (1974) advanced a theory of strategic contingencies based on Emerson's (1962) views of resource dependence, Dahl's (1957) behavioral theory of power, and Crozier's (1964) work on controlling uncertainty. According to their theory, power accrues to those departments that are able to (1) cope with organizational uncertainty, (2) perform activities that have low substitutability, and (3) perform activities that are central to the organization.

In a study designed to test the strategic contingencies theory, Hinings, Hickson, Pennings, and Schneck (1974) found statistically significant correlations between power and almost all the variables from their theory. Coping with uncertainty was the most important factor in determining power, with immediacy, non-substitutability, and pervasiveness following in that order. Additional support for strategic contingencies was provided by Salancik, Pfeffer, and Kelly (1978). Based on a study of purchasing decisions in seventeen organizations, these authors concluded that the influence of a department depended on the type of uncertainty faced and the ability of a department to reduce uncertainty.

Resource Dependence

Like strategic contingencies, resource dependence is a model of subunit power based on the work of exchange theorists (Emerson 1962, Blau 1964). According to this theory, subunits that provide critical, important, or valued resources will possess more power than other subunits (Salancik & Pfeffer 1974, Pfeffer & Salancik 1974, Pfeffer 1981b). This political model was presented as an alternative to the bureaucratic model (Baldridge 1971), which argued that work load and organizational goals were the critical factors driving organizational decisions. The resource dependence model suggests that control of resources rather than functional responsibilities or organizational rules predicts departmental power.

To test this theory, Salancik and Pfeffer (1974) examined departments in a large state university. Their findings suggest, although weakly, that departments providing resources of importance to the total organization obtain greater relative power. Specifically, they found that departments that were most able to obtain outside grants and contracts were also more influential in obtaining more of the internal budget allocations. Thus the ability to acquire outside resources facilitated the acquisition of internal resources. The authors suggest that in this instance "the rich get richer." Powerful departments are then able to secure more resources beyond those prescribed by the organizational rules.

While strategic contingencies and resource dependence perspectives are certainly the most popular approaches to intraorganizational power, they are not without serious flaws. The limitations of these perspectives are based in part on the assumptions they make concerning power in organizations and the aspects of organizational functioning which they ignore or assume away. Specific criticism will be examined in the following section.

Criticism of Critical Contingencies Perspectives

The critical contingencies theories consider power to be totally the result of subunit relationships. This view completely negates the role of history in determining power. The traditions and values of top management evolve over time and inform the political process. Clegg (1975) expresses the ahistorical criticism using a chess analogy. According to a critical contingencies view, power is like a chess game in which the pieces gain power through their current position. What this view ignores is that the power to make moves rests on the rules of the game (Clegg 1975, 49). Power according to critical contingencies theorists is determined by the environment. Power accrues to those departments in the here and now who can most easily cope with environmental constraints. Unfortunately these theorists then turn their theory around and argue that this power can be utilized to increase influence in completely different contexts. What the authors attempt to do is present an environmentally determined explanation of power and then confuse the concept of situational power by speculating that the situational power can be sustained over time.

A second criticism of these contingencies perspectives is the assumption that power is determined by uniformly agreed upon organizational goals such as survival and industry leadership while the role of subunit preferences in interpreting these organizational goals is ignored. Selznick (1957, 63) notes that leadership fails when it concentrates on survival without understanding that survival is "a matter of maintaining values and distinctive identity." It is plausible to argue that resources are viewed differently by organizational groups with conflicting values and purposes. Assuming, as Pfeffer and Salancik do, that all departments share the same values does not correspond with how organizations function. Within organizations a consistent view of goals does not exist; thus a universally agreed on view of "valued" resources or "critical" uncertainties is highly unrealistic.

Power may not be confined to the department most capable of helping the organization to align itself with the environment. For example, a powerful department may be one that supports the present policies of top management while ignoring changes in the environment. Resource dependence and strategic contingencies ignore the possibility that power may be derived from shared purposes or values. The assumption of organizational consensus or a collective mind allows these theorists to suggest that all organizational members agree on what is or isn't critical and which groups are and are not capable of controlling the unknowns.

A third criticism of the critical contingencies perspectives is the lack of attention to who defines critical contingencies or resources. It is plausible that powerful departments perpetuate their power by defining what is critical and what is not. Clearly it is not in the best interest of departments in power to note changes in contingencies when the change will decrease their influence. If the powerful get more powerful it is not because of the ability to control uncertainties as much as it is the ability to define uncertainties.

Those who have developed and tested these models rely on the perceptions and beliefs of department heads. Examination of subunits by collecting information from department heads is really an examination of managers. Hence, the research on critical contingencies represents a managerial bias. Clegg (1975) charges that this approach to power uncritically embraces management ideology and is more accurately a theory of management power. More importantly, by focusing on department heads, the critical contingencies model is clearly grounded in a social psychological as opposed to organizational perspective. The proponents of this approach treat the theory as if it were structural; however, the theory is clearly an individual exchange model for explaining managerial influence. Although they present a theory of subunit power, they measure power using the perceptions of departmental leaders. Tests of the critical contingencies model focus on interpersonal transactions that do not readily translate into a perspective for dealing with social units and their functioning.

Finally, the proponents of critical contingencies assume organizational equilibrium or a steady state. This assumption means that departmental resource control is balanced, and changes in the environment must occur to introduce uncertainty. In essence, all departments are equal until an environmental event tips the balance. Power gains are the result of imbalances in the environment that bring about disequilibrium. With the new allocation of power, this view implies that equilibrium is restored and the organization returned to the supposed prior stable state or to a new state of balance. What this assumption ignores is the possibility that departmental disequilibrium may already exist and for reasons other than environmental change. Hence other factors in the operation of the organization may be determining power relationships prior to critical environmental events.

In summary, the shortcomings of these approaches include the assumption that power is the exclusive result of department relationships and determined by one shared view of organizational goals. The lack of attention to the question of who defines critical contingencies and the excessively individual orientation in the empirical research are other weaknesses of these approaches to department power. Finally, the assumption of equilibrium or balance is a necessary beginning point for the critical contingencies argument to explain power, and this assumption is insensitive to the realities of organizational functioning.

Oftentimes an intuitively appealing theory such as the resource dependence or the strategic contingencies theory is accepted and espoused without critical examination or sufficient empirical validation. Examination of the literature indicates that these theories, while frequently discussed, have received limited empirical validation.

Empirical Support for Critical Contingencies

Empirical support for the strategic contingencies theory was first presented by the researchers whose work was noted earlier (Hinings et al. 1974). Saunders and Scamell (1982), in a replication of the Hinings et al. study, reported conflicting findings. Their data from two samples, a university and a gas company, revealed that coping with uncertainty was not as highly related to power as the other contingency variables for one sample. Non-substitutability and pervasiveness were found to be low to moderately correlated with power. These authors concluded that the relationship between power and its determinants may depend on the industry under study.

Interestingly, a recent study by Carper and Litschert (1983) of the influence of economic orientation on intraorganizational power did not find significant differences based on industry types. They conclude that an organization's economic orientation did not influence the organization's perceived power relations. While Saunders and Scamell did not find support for strategic contingencies, they did posit industry differences. The work of Carper and Litschert suggests that industry is not a critical factor in understanding intraorganizational power. The inconclusive and mixed support for a strategic contingencies theory suggests that further research is needed on the impact of context.

Since the original work by Pfeffer and Salancik, a few authors have sought to refine and extend the resource dependence theory. Hills and Mahoney (1978), for example, investigated incremental resource allocation during periods of abundance and scarcity. They concluded that during periods of scarcity powerful subunits emerge, and their power is based on external contacts. Under conditions of resource abundance, department power is not evident. The authors reason that department power emerges during periods of scarcity to protect resources, not to acquire resources.

Another elaboration of resource dependence is Daft's (1978) interest in contextual variables as factors that influence resource allocation decisions. He argues that contextual factors such as organizational size, technology, goals, and the nature of the environment facilitate or constrain resource allocation decisions. His findings supplement the resource dependence view by examining the larger organizational context, but he does not address issues of power. The results of this investigation suggest that resource allocation cannot be explained in a vacuum. Contextual factors significantly and predictably affect resource dependence.

The critical contingencies theories assume power is organized around handling critical problems, and then conclude that subunits that control the critical resources or uncertainties will gain influence in the organization.

These conclusions seem true by definition, and thus raise some doubt as to the advantage of utilizing this explanation. If power is the ability to control resources, then it seems obvious that those who control resources are powerful. The seemingly tautological nature of critical contingencies theories suggests the need for closer scrutiny of the model and further empirical examination.

The empirical support has not advanced much beyond the preliminary work. The existing research suggests mixed support for the critical contingencies theories, while offering little diversity of sample or research design to bolster support. Many of the criticisms raised in this chapter lead to the conclusion that the contingencies explanation of power is not sensitive to the role of value sharing. In the next section, the connection between value sharing and departmental influence will be explored.

Value Congruity: An Explanation of Power

Absent from the contingencies explanation of intraorganizational power is the role of values. First, organizational values serve to interpret and define the environment. Only part of the environment is an "objective" given. Environments are also enacted (Weick 1969). According to Weick (1969, 64), "the human creates the environment to which the system then adapts." Thus, at the same time an organization responds to an environment, it attempts to design it. An organization only enacts and attempts to design what it already knows (Pondy & Mitroff 1979), and values are the foundation of knowledge. Values contribute to a critical contingencies perspective by defining what the critical problems are and which departments are capable of resolving these problems (Enz 1985a).

Secondly, different subunits do not uniformly share the same organizational values. If a distinction is drawn between the organizational values of different departments, it becomes impossible to assume universal agreement on what are critical environmental factors. Thus, value differences and similarities may be contributing factors to the determination of departmental power. Groups achieve power when their values are similar to those of powerful groups (i.e. top management). Subunit power is perpetuated when a group's values are accepted and sustained.

Finally, organizations are infused with values and these shared beliefs oftentimes serve to legitimize actions or elicit commitment. Hage and Dewar (1973) observe that the beliefs of top managers are critical predictors of organizational actions. Meyer's (1982) work supports the view that the preference states of administrators guide and inform both actions and organizational structures. It follows that expressing beliefs that are consistent with the dominant group will facilitate subunit power. Beyer (1981) observes that beliefs influence decision making. Hence, it is possible that values serve as the filter for examining the environment and deciding on actions. To the extent that values play a role in organizational decisions, the power of a subunit may be directly linked to the shared organizational values. As an introduction to the literature on values some of the writing on the linkage between values and power will be reviewed. In chapters 2 and 3 the nature and facets of values and value sharing will be explored in detail.

Support for Linking Values to Power

Kaplan (1964) was one of the first theorists to write about the ways in which values relate to power in organizations. In his view, different value orientations were reflected in the different ways in which power was exercised and in the different forms of power exercised. Kaplan argued that very different approaches to power would be adopted depending on the value orientation. For example, a person who had an absolutist approach to values (i.e. absence of choice) would maintain the same absolutism in power relationships. An absolutist would use coercive power and make use of legitimacy in the form of an ideology. These rigidly held values would be used to indoctrinate everyone into understanding how things must be done. In contrast, a subjectivist would believe that values are totally personal and would rely on identification or reward power. The logic of this view is that we are all self serving and power is acquired by making others like you or like the situation. The final value orientation defined by Kaplan is the relativist view, which says that values are subjective, but grounded in the context. This orientation to values allows for a variety of approaches to power.

The view of power adopted by Kaplan relies on an examination of personal values. This orientation to values is consistent with his conceptualization of power at the interpersonal level. Although Kaplan's work focuses on the impact of specific value orientations to interpersonal power, his perspective is relevant to the present discussion of values because of his attention to the linkage between values and power. Specifically, that power is shaped by the presence of specific types of values.

At the organizational level, the works of Selznick (1957) and Stinchcombe (1968) serve as useful introductions to the role of values in the development of organizations. The work of Selznick implies that values serve as an integrating device and influence many aspects of organizational functioning. Stinchcombe conceives of organizations as having distinct values in whose service they employ resources. This author argues that social action is the result of "backing values with power" (Stinchcombe 1968, 182).

Ranson et al. (1980), while focusing on the importance of meanings in creating and recreating structure, included the impact of values on legitimating specific actions or structural frameworks. Based on a study of two hospitals, Meyer (1982) argued that shared values can serve as a substitute for formal structures. He notes that at the subunit level, value conflict can lead to dissent and debate. He concludes that mechanisms for resolving the conflicts must be institutionalized.

It seems clear that prior to the establishment of formal rules to guide value inconsistency, political power will be used. Further, the degree of congruity between the organizational leaders and the members of a subunit is likely to increase the probability that the value congruent department will wield power.

Values over time become relatively permanent aspects of the organization. To experimentally test the impact of institutionalization on social knowledge, Zucker (1977) conducted several autokinetic laboratory studies. The results of her studies reveal that social knowledge or cultural understandings were more uniform, enduring, and resistant to change when institutionalized.

Groups who influence the process of institutionalizing values legitimize their power in the process. That is, powerful groups are those that introduce and maintain values that perpetuate their power position. Specific value preferences may explain or justify a particular subunit's power. The degree to which these values are accepted by other groups is critical. If value sharing is linked with departmental power, then institutionalization of specific values will also result in the institutionalization of the subunit's power. The values will be stable, shared, and taken for granted, as will be the power relationships.

Collective definitions of acceptable behavior and desirable views are developed to reduce conflict and insure stability of the power structure in spite of environmental changes. Perpetuation of a set of values is not easy, but the process of socialization is one mechanism by which powerholders attempt to insure their values. Schein (1968) maintains that organizations socialize new members by unfreezing old values and teaching new values. Socialization is the process by which a newcomer learns the ropes, the special language, shared standards and ideology (Van Maanen and Schein 1979). To the degree that a dominant set of values are perpetuated, the possibility for subgroup revolt or dissent is limited.

Much of modern organizational theory is based on the assumption of norms of rationality (Thompson 1967). This assumption is derived from Weber's (1968) instrumentally rational type of social action. According to this scholar, instrumentally rational (formal) social action is determined by expectations about the environment and individual means for reaching rational ends. The corresponding form of authority is legal-rational, or authority based on rules and functional responsibility. In contrast, value-rational (Wertrational) social action, according to Weber, is determined by "belief in the value for its own sake" (1968, 25). While Weber does not provide a base of authority to correspond with this type of social action, recent theorists have attempted to fill this gap.

Rothschild-Whitt (1979) argues that many organizations follow from value-rational versus instrumentally rational orientations. She examines collectivist or "contrabureaucratic" organizations to illustrate that power rests in the collective rather than the individual, and is based on consensus rather than formal rules. To the extent that shared values guide the formal design of the organization, the need for political power disappears and power is shared in much the same way that values are shared.

Clearly, this extreme form of value based power is more evident in religious or ideologically focused organizations, but it is useful to understanding certain professional or entrepreneurial organizations. Value driven firms may actually lead to untraditional power relationships and organizational designs. Mintzberg (1983) reasoned that a strong ideology results in members' identification with the organization and subjugation of personal interests. He suggests that when the system of ideology is strong, other means of controlling behavior (e.g. reward and expert power) are unnecessary. This view suggests that power relationships are determined and changed by values. It is thus possible, although extremely unlikely, for political power to disappear if an organization is completely guided by a shared set of values.

While some value driven organizations may contribute to society, clearly the presence of value sharing does not automatically suggest a more humane and open organization in which power is also shared. Meyer (1982) cites the cultists at Jonestown to illustrate how a value driven organization distorted factors in the external environment. Extending his observation, this organization revolved around the personal interests of the leader, and power was clearly controlled by the leader. This is not uncommon in a value centered organization because members attach a hero status to the leader (Clark 1972).

Traditional work organizations seldom carry the value component to the extremes observed in collectivities, cults, and religious organizations. However, it is evident that organizations are both instrumentally rational (formal) and value-rational (substance). Hence, an examination of the role of values is necessary if the critical aspects of organizational functioning are to be understood.

The numerous scholars cited above lead one to conclude that values play a critical role in determining power relationships. Evidence exists to suggest that groups attempt to legitimize their power and subsequent actions by institutionalizing their values. As a result, values influence the formal authority system as well as political power relationships.

A Model of Values

My own work (Enz 1985a) provides the framework for a value sharing model to explain departmental power. The model presented in figure 1–2 indicates that the degree of congruity between departments and top management on organizationally relevant values determines which departments have power. Once a department gains power in a particular situation, it continues to exert influence in similar situations and its influence becomes institutionalized or legitimated for this particular issue over time. The shift from situational to structural power is self perpetuating as the feedback loop indicates. Thus, once a department's power is regarded as legitimate in a particular context, the department is in a better position to increase its power. Naturally, this assumes that in the process it is still value congruent with top management. Like the critical contingencies perspective, this political model of power suggests that the rich get richer.

In order for departmental power to shift, another department must espouse a set of value preferences which are more congruent with top management than are the values of other departments. Because values are prioritized, it is conceivable that the leaders' hierarchy of important organizational values may change in different situations and over time provide the impetus for shifts in department power distributions.

The linkage between power of subunits and the sharing of values with top management suggests that collectively derived preference states inform behavior. Those who share organizational preference states with the dominant coalition will gain power to control organizational functioning. The logic of this view is that top management will confer on those with "like minds" or similar understandings about the organization the opportunity to shape organizational functioning. The situational nature of this approach to power suggests that opportunities for power fall outside of the regulated authority structure and thus affect situations in which decisions to act are fraught with uncertainty, disagreement, and ambiguity. In the absence of a rule to guide behavior, those subunits with similar organizational values to the leadership will more likely gain influence. In addition, departments whose members do not agree on organizational values or departments who differ from top management on organizational values may find it difficult to gain influence in ambiguous situations.

Summary

The models of power reviewed in this chapter point to two political models. One, the contingencies model, has dominated the literature on departmental power. As the studies cited in this chapter suggest, limited support has been

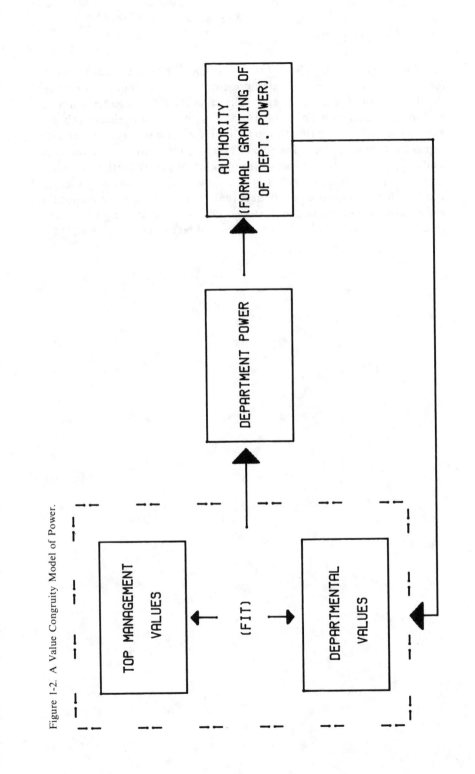

Figure 1-2. A Value Congruity Model of Power.

found for the perspective, but it continues to be a well recognized explanation for power. The cultural model presented here is another meaningful explanation of power. This approach emerges from recent attention to features of organizational culture and a recognition that established explanations for the functioning of organizations have inadequately explained people at work. The role of organizational values deserves further study. The importance of investigating value similarity further is twofold: first, the approach may conflict with popular explanations of power, and second, little empirical or conceptual work has been advanced on organizational values. In the next two chapters the existing literature on values and the nature of value congruity will be examined in detail.

2

What Are Organizational Values?

Until recently, values were absent from the rhetoric of business schools and boardrooms. The seemingly sudden interest in organizational values is due, in large part, to the presence of popular books on the subject. Peters and Waterman (1982) provide a set of guidelines for business based on their observations of successful corporations. They note, "Every excellent company we studied is clear on what it stands for, and takes the process of value shaping seriously. In fact, we wonder whether it is possible to be an excellent company without clarity on values and without having the right sorts of values" (Peters & Waterman 1982, 280). Deal and Kennedy (1982; 21, 23) observe that "often companies succeed because their employees can identify, embrace, and act on the values of the organization." These authors suggest that sharing the right organizational values will result in strong, successful organizations. Controlling, changing, or developing the corporate culture and strong shared values has been the focus of much writing in the last five years (e.g. Wilkins 1983, Allen 1985, Martin 1985).

Unfortunately, by treating organizational values as generic and by stressing how they can be controlled (manipulated), the critical nuances of sharing values is neglected. The simplistic orientation to organizational values offered by some can be dangerous. First, a "right" set of values for organizational functioning probably does not exist. Organizations that try to develop values that appear right but do not match the firm can create serious problems rather than solve problems. This is not to say that similar values do not exist across organizations. Extremely different firms may have similar values, but there is no ideal set of organizational values. In addition, developing a strong set of values can lead to stagnation and inflexibility. Thus, value sharing can be dysfunctional when the values are imposed rather than emergent and when the need for value changes are ignored. It is possible that sharing values produces myopic decision making and poor adaptation, not success.

Nevertheless, to function in an organization, employees must do more than possess the necessary skills and abilities, follow the rules, and work a full day. To participate in the organization's activities, individuals must also learn what the organization's leaders value. This knowledge helps workers to know what to do in situations of uncertainty or instances when the formal rules and procedures do not clearly dictate actions. The role that organizational values play is one of guiding choices and providing meaning to various actions and goals. These values typically work in harmony with the formal structures to dictate behaviors. Values will change over time, but slowly, and they will usually reflect the guiding principles of top management.

What are organizational values? While the term value is bounced about frequently, few have taken the time to clarify or sharpen the term. Perry (1931) mused many years ago that we can tell scholars' areas of study by the words they use carefully and the words they use carelessly. The present literature in organizational studies clearly does not regard the term value as one of its careful words.

The difficulty in discussing values is that many tend to use values as an adjective or verb in normal conversation. We are likely to hear people make remarks such as, "I value your opinion" or "The valued resource was money." These examples refer to the activity of placing value on something. It is necessary to distinguish between "that which is desired" and "that which is desirable" (see Williams 1960 for a discussion of this issue). Values are not things we desire or want; rather, they are conceptions of the desirable. Values are standards, preferences, or criteria established to determine desirability (Kluckholn 1956, Williams 1960, Rokeach 1968).

Given the many common-sense meanings for values, it is essential that we take time to treat the concept of values carefully. Hence, it is necessary to depart from the popular literature at this point and begin to sharpen and clarify what organizational values are and are not. The practitioner literature suggests in an illustrative and anecdotal fashion that values are perhaps the most important ingredient to organizational functioning. To investigate the viability of this claim, it is necessary to first develop and refine a definition of organizational values.

The nature and definition of organizational values will be explored in this chapter. Findings will be presented from a study of two companies, focusing specifically on describing and categorizing organizational values shared among the companies' employees. In the latter portion of the chapter the values of top management will be presented along with a discussion of the role executives play in shaping and forming values. The purpose of examining the specific substantive values of individuals in two organizations is to determine if some universal organizational values exist, as perceived by different individuals and top managers.

Definitional Clarity or Muddying the Waters?

Sloppy terminology and fuzzy conceptualization pervade the work on values, as noted above. This problem is confounded by the lack of precision in identifying the reference for discussions of values. Personal values, work values and organizational values tap different components of the process and, while interrelated, they are also distinct. The present approach to values stresses secular not religious values, work related not global values, and organizational not job centered or personal values. Approaches that concentrate on beliefs about an individual's job (Wollack et al. 1971) or universal values (Withey 1965, Scott 1965, Bales & Couch 1969) are not appropriate for this investigation. Central to the discussion here are the preferences for how organizations should be run.

The numerous value studies in the social sciences have concentrated on individual values (those values held by a person in a broad social context) and work values (those values concerning performance on the job). Organizational values are centered in the organization as the cultural milieu and are concerned with preferences for what the company should do. The specific reference for the study of organizational values is not the individual or the job, but the corporation. The important question for investigating organizational values is, what actions and goals should the group of persons in this organization select as the most desirable?

Examples of typical personal values would include religiousness, self-control, and kindness (Scott 1965). Work values have included pride in work, job involvement, and upward striving (Wallack 1971). Organizational values include industry leadership, profits, and creative product development (Enz 1985a). As evidenced by the examples, the substance of different conceptualizations of values underscores the distinctiveness of the multiple levels at which values are explored.

Another point of confusion rests with the tendency to use the term values loosely and as a synonym for similar aspects of the informal organization. Within the organizational culture literature, depending on the author's personal preferences, the terms value, belief, ideology, style, shared meaning, saga, mission and culture are used to mean the same thing. Confusion is further heightened by the popularity of the term in a variety of different fields. Within the disciplines of philosophy, psychology, sociology, economics, anthropology, and organizational studies, the term value is used with some degree of specificity. A brief list of some common definitions of the term in different disciplines is presented in table 2-1.

Philosophers define the term in many different ways; some separate values (good and bad) from ethics (right and wrong); others do not draw this

Table 2-1.   Definitions of Values.

Philosophy
>   "...a thing—any thing—has value, or is valuable, in the original and generic sense when it is the object of an interest—any interest."
>
>   (Perry 1954, 2–3)

Economics
>   "The word value . . . has two different meanings, and sometimes expresses the utility of some particular object, and sometimes the power of purchasing other goods which the possession of that object conveys."
>
>   (Smith 1776, 131)

Comparative Cross-Cultural Studies
>   "...a broad tendency to prefer certain states of affairs over others."
>
>   (Hofstede 1984, 18)

Psychology
>   "A value is an enduring belief that a specific mode of conduct or end-state of existence is personally or socially preferable to an opposite or converse mode of conduct or end-state of existence."
>
>   (Rokeach 1968, 5)

Sociology / Anthropology
>   "A value is a conception, explicit or implicit, distinctive of an individual or characteristic of a group, of the desirable which influences the selection from available modes, means, and ends of action."
>
>   (Kluckhohn 1967, 395)

Organizational Studies
>   "Values refer to preferences for courses of action and outcomes."
>
>   (Beyer 1981, 167)

---

distinction. Economists use the term value in a precise and specific fashion dating back to Adam Smith and the value theory of economics. Sociology, anthropology and psychology are comparative newcomers to the investigation of values, and approach the concept differently; yet some degree of similarity pervades the use of the term within these disciplines. Values have been treated as generalized meanings (Kluckholn 1967); unconscious assumptions (Homans 1950); mental programs (Hofstede 1984); and preferences (Rokeach 1968).

Rose (1956) distinguishes between the philosophers' and economists' views of values (who treat values as givens), and the orientations of the sociologists, anthropologists and psychologists (who explore the antecedents and consequences of values). This distinction is useful for the present examination of values, which does not take values as givens and then proceed with other questions, but rather explores specifically the consequences for organizational life of sharing values.

Attempts to devise a workable definition of values, excluding the discussions in the popular literature, reveal a surprising degree of definitional convergence in the social sciences. Two primary components are evident in most definitions of values. First, the definition focuses attention on means and ends or actions and goals. Secondly, values are viewed as preferences, or priorities. By combining these two components we have a definition that suggests that values are viewed as preferences for or the priority of certain goals and actions (Kluckholn 1967, Rose 1956, Rokeach 1968). The emphasis of these definitions is on desirability and oughtness and stresses selection from among different means and end states (Brown 1976, Rokeach 1968, Schmidt and Posner 1982). Values are the beliefs a group of persons express by preference in the context of identifying desirable courses of action and goals (ends).

Organizational values, in particular, are beliefs held by an individual or group that speak to the actions and goals (ends) organizations "ought to" or "should" identify in the running of the enterprise. Organizational values specify which business actions or objectives are preferable to alternate actions or corporate objectives.

The perspective on values developed in sociology, organizational studies, psychology and anthropology emphasizes beliefs as prescriptive or proscriptive. Sproull (1981) calls this category of beliefs normative or preferred states of being. Beliefs can be categorized as evaluative (right or wrong), descriptive (true or false) or prescriptive (preferred states), but a value to Sproull refers only to prescriptive beliefs. Emphasis is placed on actions (means) and goals (ends). Beyer's (1981) approach to values is similar in that she focuses on values as normative standards or preferences for certain actions or outcomes. The definition favored here reflects the common features of prior definitions and views organizational values as the preferences for or the desirability of certain courses of action within the enterprise or certain outcomes for the firm.

Numerous researchers and theorists have used the means/ends conceptualization of values (Kluckholn 1951, Hillard 1950, Rokeach 1968, Beyer 1981). Means refer to the course of action taken by an organization, and ends are the goals or outcomes. Clearly values which deal with actions and those that deal with goals are interrelated. At the present stage of theoretical development there is little evidence to suggest that actions and goals are distinct and separable (see Rokeach 1968 for a conflicting view on distinctiveness). An organizational value designated as a goal (e.g. profits) may be considered a means to an ultimate goal (such as survival). For this reason the present approach to values will combine actions and goals (means/ends) conceptualizations of values.

The Characteristics of Values

The nature of values suggests that they are long lasting and pervasive, but capable of being changed. Values are derived from both the social context and the organizationally specific context; that is, they are culturally imposed. Mannheim (1936, 82) notes that values are unintelligible unless they are examined "with reference to the concrete situations to which they have relevance and in which they are valid." Values serve as a criterion or standard for guiding behavior, and in this context influence perceptions (England 1975), provide rationalizations for socially unacceptable behavior (Rokeach 1968), provide organization (Adler 1956), and rationalize power inequalities (Kamens 1977). Values guide attitudes and behaviors in a pattern much like the one suggested below. This diagram emphasizes the centrality of values suggesting that they are broad and inform both perceptions and actions.

Values ——> Attitudes ——> Behaviors

As Perry (1931) noted, values combine the specific reference with breadth and flexibility. Values are cultural products which inform our attitudes and actions (Allport 1961, Rokeach 1978, Woodruff 1942). By cultural products it is suggested that values are learned rather than inherited or instinctual. Individuals within a firm learn the organizational values through interaction with others. They also bring to the organization values learned earlier in their lives. Because of the heterogeneity of the societal culture, individuals will share some values in common with many fellow employees and other values with subgroups within the work force (Enz 1985b). In the process of acclimating to the organization, workers learn to integrate the values they possess and those taught in the organizational context into a preference ordering. The process of prioritizing different organizational values sets the stage for value sharing as well as value conflicts.

Talcott Parsons is perhaps the best known of the sociologists who utilized a value orientation to explain the functioning of social organizations. According to Parsons, value consensus is the critical ingredient in shaping and controlling social structures. He stressed that, "all values involve what may be called a social reference . . . they are cultural rather than purely personal; they are in fact shared" (Parsons 1964, 12). In this view, cultural values determine the shaping of social systems. Values are learned and shared among individuals and provide the basis for defining and making sense of social structures. The process of institutionalization for Parsons is the structuring of value orientations in the social system. Values add meaning and regularity to the patterning of actions.

Parsons and Shils (1967) observe that values have three components: the cognitive, the emotional (cathectic), and the evaluative. Simply, the possession of a value suggests that the individual thinks about what is desirable, has an emotional attachment to what is desirable, and determines desirability from among a group of possible actions and goals. Kluckholn (1967, 396) argues that a value is "not just a preference," but it is "felt" and/or "considered to be justified." Therefore, values are a blend of thoughts, feelings, and preferences.

A common critique of Parsons is the dangerous assumption of consensus in values. The potential within an organization for different groups to function with distinct and conflicting sets of values is readily acknowledged in this analysis of values. Clearly, different subgroups within organizations develop their own sets of common values. The literature on subcultures and groups indirectly provides support for the view that members of a particular group because of proximity, interpersonal attraction, affiliation, and other factors oftentimes shared values that are unique to the group and differ from the values of persons in other groups (Shaw 1981). The work of Lawrence and Lorsch (1968) highlights the distinctiveness of functional departments within organizations. These authors empirically examined the degree to which functional units operated with different cognitive and emotional orientations (differentiation). They emphasized the importance that division of labor plays in shaping the orientations of different departments within organizations.

In the last two sections we have examined the numerous definitions of values and the nature of values. It is assumed that organizational values are preference states that are culturally based, pervasive and enduring, but capable of being changed. Values influence how organizations are designed and are not uniformly shared by all subgroups within an organization. In particular, different functional departments for a variety of reasons may operate with distinct sets of values. Finally, the focus for study is on organizational values or values that are unique to a particular business and that reflect the preferences for how that company should be run.

The Substance of Organizational Values

While discussion of organizational values in the abstract is of theoretical and conceptual interest, attaching some substance to the label organizational values is also necessary. In the following section, interviews with 81 persons in two companies will be summarized to determine what specific categories of values are frequently mentioned by organizational participants. In addition, the findings of two surveys involving 412 people will provide some indication of how different groups of people prioritize different organizational values.

What are the most important organizational values to various groups of workers? To answer this question, two different organizations were selected for study. Roboto (a fictional name), a young high technology company located in the Midwest was selected as one company for study. The second organization, Food King (a fictional name), is a national fast food company with corporate headquarters in the Midwest. Food King is considered one of the fastest growing and most innovative restaurant chains. Roboto is a venture capital company that specializes in one application for metal treatment within the robotics industry.

The organizations were selected because of their size and diversity of work unit activities. Selecting small organizations allowed for examination of each corporate department and insured that employees were reasonably familiar with the activities of various departments. In addition, every employee had some familiarity or contact with top management. For a detailed discussion of the methodology employed in conducting the study on which this and additional findings reported in this book are based see appendix A.

Important Organizational Values

Values considered most important by employees in a particular organization are those which are mutually identified by a group and thus arise in part from social interaction. It is the organizationally shared values that people must deal with and toward which they develop their work related actions. It follows that in order to understand people's actions it is necessary to identify the values most often emphasized.

By transcribing eighty-one interviews and coding interview responses, the frequency with which different values were mentioned was ascertained. Tables 2-2 and 2-3 present lists of consistently mentioned values for Food King and Roboto respectively. These responses are to a series of open-ended questions regarding what the interviewee thinks a company should value in running its business. Appendix B provides a list of questions used during the interview stage of the study reported here. The questions in the interviews dealt with power and critical contingencies issues as well as specific questions regarding organizational values. Responses to interview questions were used to develop and customize value items asked later in a survey of all employees.

Table 2-2.   The Most Important Values a Company Should Have.

(Frequency of Open-Ended Response for Food King)

VALUE STATEMENTS	FREQUENCY OF RESPONSE*	
	n	%
Employees (People)	36	75.00%
Ethics (Honesty, Integrity, Morality)	20	41.67%
Customers	17	35.42%
Community Involvement	15	31.25%
Profits	14	29.17%
Product (Quality, Service, Cleanliness)	13	27.08%
A Philosophy to Guide	7	14.58%
Image (Reputation)	6	12.50%
Creativity / Innovation	6	12.50%
Strategic Planning (Direction)	5	10.42%
Communication	4	8.33%
Professionalism	3	6.25%
Flexibility	3	6.25%
High Performance Standards	2	4.17%
Good Physical Facilities	2	4.17%
Credibility	1	2.08%
Aggressiveness	1	2.08%
Good Franchisees	1	2.08%
Having Fun	1	2.08%

*The responses are multiple ones and therefore will not total 100%.

Nineteen different values were mentioned by the forty-eight people interviewed in Food King. Seventeen distinct values emerged from the twenty-nine persons in Roboto who were interviewed. The most important values for running a business involved people, ethics, and customers in Food King and people, product reliability, and integrity in Roboto. These most frequently cited values will be explored individually.

Value People

In both companies, the most frequently mentioned item a company should value was people. A closer examination of responses revealed that valuing people could be categorized into three themes: (1) the employer's philosophy of dealing with employees, (2) the employer's actions toward employees, and

Table 2-3.   The Most Important Values a Company Should Have.

(Frequency of Open-Ended Response for Roboto)

VALUE STATEMENTS	FREQUENCY OF RESPONSE*	
	n	%
Support of People / Concern for People	19	65.52%
Reliable Product You Stand Behind	13	44.83%
Integrity / Honesty / Morality	13	44.83%
Customers	7	24.14%
Support From Investors	5	17.24%
Technological Advancements	4	13.79%
Profit	4	13.79%
Good Strategic Plan / Stick To The Plan	4	13.79%
A Philosophy	3	10.34%
Company Image (Reputation)	3	10.34%
Professionalism	1	6.90%
Dedication / Loyalty To Company	1	6.90%
Good Morale	1	6.90%
Good Work Environment	1	6.90%
Ability To Monitor Company Performance	1	6.90%
Team Atmosphere	1	6.90%
Selecting Qualified People	1	6.90%

*The responses are multiple ones and therefore will not total 100%.

(3) the employee's responsibilities. Table 2-4 summarizes the three people-valuing themes.

Most respondents stressed the first theme concerning an employer's philosophy of dealing with employees. Regarding people as valuable versus expendable was at the heart of a philosophy for treating people as an asset. An employer's philosophy should include believing in people, listening to them regardless of formal position, and trusting them. Food King personnel focused on issues of respect and equity while Roboto respondents emphasized trust. As one Roboto employee noted,

> We need a reason to believe in the company. Management should treat the worker as important. If you treat people right, you get loyalty. Value your people and everything else comes.

The second theme stressed how a company acts toward its employees. This area of valuing people stressed selection, training, wages and development as central components. A company should recruit the "right kind of people." One Food King manager defined the right people as "people

Table 2-4.   Themes for Valuing People.

CATEGORIES	FOOD KING	ROBOTO
Employer Philosophy	Regarding people as valuable vs. expendable.	Believing people grow.
	Being people oriented.	Treating people as assets vs. expendable resources.
	Treating people with dignity and respect.	Having faith in employees.
	Equity, do not discriminate based on level in the organization.	Be honest with employees and communicate.
		Trust all employees, listen to people.
Employer Actions	Responsibilities of the Company concerning employee development, training, selection, and pay.	Recognize individual accomplishments.
	Communicating with people.	Selecting good people.
	Flexibility, allowing mistakes.	Holding on to people with experience.
	Taking care of employees.	Keeping high achievers.
		Concern for employees' well-being.
Responsible Employees	Dedication Trustworthy	Pride Commitment
	Enthusiasm	

who understand what we are trying to do and believe in it." The right kind of people are those who are willing to work for the company and believe in what the company is doing. Fair compensation and support of employee development were areas that interviewees felt companies should value.

The third theme of valuing people concentrated on the employee's responsibility to be dedicated and trustworthy. It was felt by many interviewed that loyalty to a company was a natural outcome of a company philosophy that regarded people as assets and treated people with consideration. This aspect of attaching value to employees emphasized the role which the employee must play in the process of valuing. Workers should in effect value the company and thus exhibit commitment and dedication. Those interviewed were extremely intolerant of employees who did not support the company and encourage long run success. While a company should place a high priority on considering its employees, the employees interviewed also felt the worker must place an equally high priority on company success.

A card sort activity conducted during the interviews yielded findings similar to the open-ended questions, while narrowing the importance of specific facets of the treatment of people. Interviewees were provided 27 cards with a value on each card. The individual was asked to read the value statement and then sort the values into piles according to his preferences. Based on the card sort it was discovered that valuing people centered on communication (in both companies) and employee development (for Food King only), but employee welfare, satisfaction, and cohesiveness were rarely selected as important values. This finding suggests that valuing people centers on work related actions and interactions, not general affect issues. Many persons believe that if the work related issues are valued, satisfaction and cohesiveness will follow.

Value Ethics and Honesty

Companies should be ethical and honest according to the employees interviewed. Integrity and morality in the operation of a business were the second most frequently mentioned values a company should have. While both companies' employees considered ethics to be critical, employees at Food King thought top management was illustrative of integrity and honesty. Numerous references were made to the ethical and religious commitment of the executives. The president and founder was viewed as the force behind and shaper of the company's ethics. One employee referred to the sense of integrity as "keeping the promise." Another employee noted the values of Food King are the values of the president, when you join the organization you "sign on [to that set of values] and you believe it." A company needs to stand for something significant, according to the employees of Food King. "When a company stops believing in integrity and morality they become cutthroat and profit centered," noted one worker.

Religion was a theme that could not be overlooked in this firm. The Christian beliefs of the founder had a profound effect on how workers viewed the company. Many could not imagine how the company would wrong them since the founder was a religious man. Whether he could or would is irrelevant; they believed he would not. Trust in the company was not total in

Food King. People in some departments viewed Food King as "too nice" and felt that more aggressive actions, cutting corners, and less consideration of personnel would improve the profitability of the company. Others in middle management felt trapped in a set of values that prevented the organization from growing.

In contrast, Roboto top management was consistently cited for the absence of integrity and ethical standards. Integrity in dealing with customers and employees was a central value issue for those in Roboto. Numerous interviewees cited the same example of perceived top management dishonesty to illustrate their opinions. Conducting business responsibly and putting integrity behind the product were strong preferences for the respondents. Many expressed the opinion that the company fell short of these ethical values and was opportunistic, not ethical. Once again the chief executive was considered the primary person responsible for delineating the values and setting an example. Dishonesty was felt to have turned employees into cynics. Every change in policy was construed as a manipulative action by the executive.

Interestingly, the importance of ethics as a primary organizational value was highlighted in both firms even though the value was represented in the behaviors of executives in Food King and absent from the actions of the management of Roboto. This observation suggests that when the organizational leaders do not adopt or act on a value, the value will not be reflected in organizational actions, even if a large percentage of employees espouse the particular value. A value conflict is likely to exist and may indicate instability and ambiguity in organizational functioning.

Close examination of Roboto revealed that dissent and debate frequently surfaced on issues and actions that were described as unethical by some groups of organizational participants. While the dominate values of top management guided actions, conflict was prevalent and often led back to a fundamental difference regarding what the company should do in specific situations.

Value the Customer

The customer, in the eyes of many, should be valued above all else. Valuing the customer was the third most popular value stated in the open-ended portion of the interviews. As one employee noted, "The customer should come first." A company should value customer satisfaction, according to a worker at Food King. Fair dealings with customers were stressed by persons in Roboto. Maintaining a relationship with customers, supporting the customer after delivery of the product, and giving the customer what he expects were facets of valuing customers according to those in Roboto.

Probes to determine the commitment of employees to this principle revealed far greater conviction than had been anticipated. Far from being a cliché, the employees demonstrated strong beliefs in customer service. Examples and stories were used to illustrate the level of commitment to this value.

Value Profits and Products

In addition to the three most frequently mentioned values a company should have, profits and products were also noted. Surprisingly, the importance of profits was often acknowledged by persons in staff areas such as personnel. In contrast, persons in typically money oriented departments such as finance did not mention the importance of profits. Products and product quality were cited by many persons, but usually stressed by those in operations and engineering areas. The tendency of these employees to stress products is consistent with what one would expect in departments that focus on product delivery and development.

Roboto and Food King, while very dissimilar in industrial and environmental factors, shared many similar values. It is interesting to find that the continually emphasized set of values is not substantially altered when studying organizations with different characteristics. Keeping in mind that these are preference statements, not reflections of "reality," it is not too surprising that employees express some common values. This observation is consistent with the findings of Posner and Schmidt (1984), who noted in their study that strong agreement on values existed among managers in different organizations. They referred to this value similarity as a "managerial psyche." In the organizations examined here, the psyche appears to differ by departments.

Organizational and Departmental Differences

Within both organizations differences in the priorities of values were observed. All the employees in the two companies studied were asked to rank order a list of 24 value statements developed in the interviews. Almost 500 employees ranked their organizational values. Examination of the value rankings for each company (see tables 2–5 and 2–6) reveals that differences between the companies exist. For Food King, the important organizational values were superior quality and service, professionalism, ethics, efficiency, and profits, in that order. Roboto personnel selected superior quality and service, professionalism, survival, industry leadership and ethics. Examining the ordering of the list of values indicates a different prioritizing.

Table 2-5. Frequency of Value Ranking for Food King.
(N = 356)

VALUE	RANKED #1 %	RANKED #2 %	RANKED #3 %
SUPERIOR QUALITY & SERVICE	36.2%	16.8%	8.7%
PROFESSIONALISM	11.9%	6.5%	7.8%
ETHICS	11.9%	7.6%	6.3%
EFFICIENCY	4.9%	12.8%	8.7%
PROFITS	4.0%	3.1%	5.6%
OPEN COMMUNICATION	3.6%	3.8%	5.8%
AGGRESSIVENESS	3.4%	3.1%	5.4%
HIGH MORALE	3.4%	7.2%	8.5%
COMPANY GROWTH	2.7%	4.9%	5.1%
INDUSTRY LEADERSHIP	2.2%	2.2%	1.3%
EMPLOYEE DEVELOPMENT	2.0%	3.6%	7.8%
SURVIVAL	2.0%	.7%	.7%
COMMUNITY INVOLVEMENT	1.8%	5.4%	3.4%
CREATIVITY	1.8%	4.5%	4.5%
COMPANY INDIVIDUALITY	1.3%	2.9%	2.9%
COMPANY STABILITY	1.1%	2.0%	1.6%
ADAPTABILITY	1.1%	2.0%	4.0%
EMPLOYEE SATISFACTION	.9%	4.5%	3.8%
SOCIAL WELL BEING	.2%	1.1%	1.1%
LOW TURNOVER	.2%	.9%	1.6%
CREATIVE PRODUCT DEVELOPEMENT	.2%	1.3%	1.6%
SUPPORT FAILURES	0.0%	0.0%	.2%
REDUCED LABOR COSTS	0.0%	0.0%	.2%
CONTROL OVER THE ENVIRONMENT	0.0%	0.0%	0.0%

This analysis serves to extend the preliminary interview findings by getting more workers involved in evaluating their value preferences. In addition to organizational differences, value ordering differed by departments within the two organizations.

Individuals in different departments stressed different values. The differing value orientations of respondents in different departments is consistent with the concept of differentiation defined by Lawrence and Lorsch (1967).

To illustrate the department differences, tables 2–7 and 2–8 provide the five most frequently mentioned values by department. The ranking activity suggests that department differences do exist in prioritizing, but a remarkably similar overall list of values exists. Clearly, superior quality and service was

Table 2-6.   Frequency of Value Ranking for Roboto.
(N = 56)

VALUE	RANKED #1 %	RANKED #2 %	RANKED #3 %
SUPERIOR QUALITY & SERVICE	39.7%	20.7%	10.3%
PROFESSIONALISM	12.1%	8.6%	1.7%
SURVIVAL	10.3%	1.7%	1.7%
INDUSTRY LEADERSHIP	8.6%	8.6%	1.7%
ETHICS	6.9%	12.1%	6.9%
AGGRESSIVENESS	5.2%	0	5.2%
EFFICIENCY	5.2%	5.2%	8.6%
HIGH MORALE	3.4%	1.7%	10.3%
CREATIVITY	1.7%	3.4%	5.2%
COMPANY STABILITY	1.7%	3.4%	3.4%
PROFITS	1.7%	6.9%	3.4%
CREATIVE PRODUCT DEVELOPMENT	1.7%	3.4%	6.9%
OPEN COMMUNICATION	1.7%	1.7%	6.9%
EMPLOYEE SATISFACTION	0	6.9%	3.4%
ADAPTABILITY	0	3.4%	5.2%
EMPLOYEE DEVELOPMENT	0	5.2%	1.7%
SOCIAL WELL BEING	0	1.7%	0
SUPPORT FAILURES	0	1.7%	5.2%
COMPANY GROWTH	0	3.4%	10.3%
LOW TURNOVER	0	0	1.7%
CONTROL OVER THE ENVIRONMENT	0	0	0
COMMUNITY INVOLVEMENT	0	0	0
COMPANY INDIVIDUALITY	0	0	0
REDUCED LABOR COSTS	0	0	0

regarded as the most important value. Superior quality means the ability to make a good product and address all the needs of the customer in a fast and friendly manner.

For Food King, the organizational values that were stressed by operations personnel focused on product and people issues. In contrast, the personnel and training functions expressed preferences for company growth and ethics. Marketing groups valued professionalism and growth. As the most important value, product quality and service was a solid theme.

In Roboto, the engineering groups valued professionalism, creativity, and leadership. Manufacturing frequently mentioned efficiency, and personnel stressed survival. Unlike Food King, the value rankings did not suggest a clear central value, but rather the presence of two strong priorities, including survival and product quality.

In sum, a few values appeared to surface across departments, yet others were specific to a department. For example, in Food King, an overarching

Table 2-7. Food King Departmental Values.
(Five most frequently mentioned values for each department)

DEPARTMENT	RANKED 1	RANKED 2	RANKED 3	RANKED 4	RANKED 5
FINANCE	Quality & Service	Ethics	Aggressiveness	Efficiency	Profits
LEGAL	Quality & Service	Efficiency	Ethics	Open Communication	Adaptability
MARKETING	Quality & Service	Co. Stability	Professionalism	High Morale	Social Well
TRAINING	Ethics	Quality & Service	Co. Growth	Open Communication	Profits
PERSONNEL	Ethics	Quality & Service	Community Activity	Survival	Co. Growth
SALES	Profits	Professionalism	Ethics	Quality & Service	Industry Leader
DEVELOPMENT	Creativity	Quality & Service	Professionalism	Co. Growth	Creativity
PURCHASING	Quality & Service	Profits	Open Communication	Co. Growth	Professionalism
STORES	Quality & Service	High Morale	Ethics	Profits	High Morale
DISTRICTS	Quality & Service	High Morale	Employee Development	Open Communication	Co. Growth
REGION A	Quality & Service	Ethics	Professionalism	Employee Development	Efficiency
REGION B	Quality & Service	Co. Growth	Professionalism	Profits	Satisfaction
REGION C	Quality & Service	Creativity	Efficiency	Professionalism	Ethics
CORP. OPERATIONS	Quality & Service	Efficiency	Professionalism	Ethics	Community Activity

LEVEL OF MANAGEMENT

	RANKED 1	RANKED 2	RANKED 3	RANKED 4	RANKED 5
TOP	Profits	Ethics	Quality & Service	Co. Growth	Satisfaction
MIDDLE	Quality & Service	Profits	Ethics	Co. Growth	Professionalism
LOWER	Quality & Service	Professionalism	Ethics	Efficiency	High Morale

Table 2-8. Roboto Departmental Values.
(Five most frequently mentioned values for each department)

DEPARTMENT	RANKED 1	RANKED 2	RANKED 3	RANKED 4	RANKED 5
FINANCE	Survival	Aggressiveness	Efficiency	Ethics	Co. Growth
PERSONNEL	Survival	Aggressiveness	Profits	Quality & Service	Ethics
MANUF. MATL.	Survival	Quality & Service	Profits	Efficiency	Ethics
MANUF. ELECT.	Quality & Service	Efficiency	High Morale	Open Communication	Low Turnover
MANUF. MECH.	Ethics	Quality & Service	Aggressiveness	Efficiency	Open Communication
MANUF. GENERAL	Industry Leader	Quality & Service	Adaptability	Satisfaction	Open Communication
QUALITY CONTROL	High Morale	Quality & Service	Creative Products	Employee Development	Support Failures
SALES	Quality & Service	Industry Leader	Ethics	Adaptability	Creative Products
MKT. APPLIC.	Quality & Service	Ethics	Co. Growth	Aggressiveness	Profits
MARKETING	Open Communication	Quality & Service	Adaptability	Creative Products	Employee Development
CUSTOMER SERVICE	Quality & Service	Efficiency	Open Communication	Satisfaction	Survival
SOFTWARE ENG.	Quality & Service	Professionalism	Creativity	Aggressiveness	Efficiency
DEVELOPMENT	Quality & Service	Ethics	Creativity	Survival	Satisfaction
PRODUCT ENG.	Quality & Service	Professionalism	Industry Leader	Efficiency	Co. Growth
ENG. GENERAL	Quality & Service	Professionalism	Industry Leader	Ethics	High Morale

LEVEL OF MANAGEMENT

	RANKED 1	RANKED 2	RANKED 3	RANKED 4	RANKED 5
TOP	Profits	Industry Leader	Quality & Service	Ethics	Survival
MIDDLE	Quality & Service	Adaptability	Open Communication	Efficiency	Profits
PROFESSIONAL	Quality & Service	Industry Leader	Survival	Ethics	Professionalism
LOWER	Quality & Service	Professionalism	Efficiency	Co. Stability	High Morale

organizational value is clearly quality and service. Aggressiveness, creativity, employee satisfaction, community activity and other values emerged in some departments' lists of critical preferences but did not surface in other departments.

Level of Management

Throughout the interview process, personnel at different levels of the organization stressed different values. In the interviews, those in lower levels at Roboto and Food King stressed people issues, whereas those in middle management positions concentrated on profits, technological and product advances, and customer needs. At the top management level, the desirability of supporting and encouraging people became a dominate theme again. Differences based on position in the organization were not strong, but were present.

Examination of survey findings (see tables 2–7 and 2–8) revealed some contradictory opinions, particularly from the top management team. In interviews top managers spent large blocks of time discussing employee related values, but consistently ranked profits as most important when taking a survey. Middle managers mentioned profits, but did not rank it as most important. Lower level managers did not mention profits, but stressed morale and company stability. These findings raise some doubt as to whether top management was candid in the interviews. Possibly the social undesirability of stressing profits explains their tendency to avoid mentioning profits in face to face contact. Middle managers, in contrast, were very open about what they valued, and argued that top management did share these values. Evidence from the survey supports the claims of these managers to a much greater extent than one-on-one interviews. Many subordinates indicated that top management was more interested in money and growth than in people. Hence, it is possible that the survey rankings of values is a better indicator of top management views.

Least Important Values

The respondents from the two companies showed less agreement when selecting unimportant values. Unimportant values are those values that are the least desirable for a company to consider when running a business. Identification of undesirable values was far more difficult a task, with the notable exception of controlling the environment and reducing labor costs. The ability to influence things that happen outside an organization that impact on what happens inside an organization, and the ability to reduce the cost of employing workers were two values regarded as undesirable. Strong agreement across organizations existed regarding the undesirability of controlling the environment and reducing labor costs.

A summary of the card sort of least important values is provided in table 2–9. Based on the frequencies, Food King's employees selected survival, company individuality, and industry leadership as unimportant values. The individuals in Roboto cited social well-being, profit maximization, and low turnover as unimportant values.

The undesirability of controlling the environment is of considerable interest since a large body of literature in organizational theory concentrates on how organizations devote time and money to influencing things that happen outside their boundaries. This literature also stresses the desirability of controlling the environment. Over fifty percent of the respondents indicated that control of the environment was the least desirable of all value statements. Most respondents noted that people, the customer, and ethical behavior were more important preferences than trying to control the environment. Many expressed the view that in competitive industries, organizations cannot control the environment (e.g. customers, suppliers, competition) and more important, they should not try. Both companies agreed that reduced labor costs were not important to value, but did not agree on the undesirability of any of the other organizational values.

Once again, within Roboto and Food King departmental differences existed. For example, in one company finance felt sales growth was the least important value and marketing felt it was the most important value. Operations felt creative product development was unimportant while the legal department of the same company felt that employee cohesiveness was not important to value. Engineering in one company felt profit and creativity were not desirable while finance and marketing stressed social well-being.

Clearly, top management is a critical group in examining values because of its control over organizational design and functioning. To understand the role of values in an organizational context requires close examination of the organizational leaders and how their beliefs operate to influence the activities within the firm.

Top Managers as the Value Makers

There is a tendency for some who study organizations to attribute behaviors or actions to organizations. While reification has long been recognized as a possible problem in studying organizations, the alternative of reductionism has never satisfactorily solved the problem. Yes, organizations are composed of individuals and, literally speaking, the organization does not behave or have values. However, we are aware of patterns of behavior within organizations that are repeated even though the individual actors change. We

Table 2-9.   Least Important Values a Company Should Have.
(Frequency of Response to Card Sort)

VALUES	FREQUENCY OF RESPONSE*			
	Food King		Roboto	
	n	%	n	%
	(n=41)		(n=29)	
Control over the Environment	22	53.66%	17	58.62%
Survival	21	51.22%	4	13.79%
Reduced Labor Costs	20	48.79%	11	37.93%
Company Individuality	18	43.90%	8	27.59%
Industry Leadership	18	43.90%	6	20.69%
Employee Cohesiveness	14	34.15%	7	24.14%
Company Stability	12	29.27%	4	13.79%
Aggressiveness	8	19.51%	6	20.69%
Profit Maximization	8	19.51%	11	37.93%
High Productivity	7	17.07%	6	20.69%
Having Fun	7	19.07%	8	27.59%
Low Turnover	6	14.63%	10	34.48%
Creative Product Development	6	14.63%	1	3.45%
Adaptability	5	12.20%	4	13.79%
Growth in Sales	5	12.20%	4	13.79%
Social Well Being	4	9.76%	12	41.38%
Professionalism	4	9.76%	2	6.90%
Open Communication	3	7.32%	0	00%
High Morale	3	7.32%	0	00%
Employee Satisfaction	3	7.32%	3	10.35%
Creativity	3	7.32%	3	10.35%
Superior Service	3	7.32%	1	3.45%
Employee Welfare	2	4.89%	3	10.35%
Superior Quality	2	4.89%	0	00%
Morality	2	4.89%	0	00%
Company Growth	1	2.44%	3	10.35%
Employee Development	1	2.44%	4	13.79%

*The responses are multiple ones and therefore will not total 100%.

also know that organizational values are shared and endure, while individual members come and go.

The strategic management literature has long recognized the central role and tremendous impact the CEOs and top executives have on the direction and mission of the firm (Andrews 1980, Lorange 1980). *Fortune* magazine and *Business Week* regularly make reference to those leaders who define or redefine the nature and functioning of the enterprise. Books about such men as Henry Ford III, Lee Iacocca, Harold Geneen or Jean Riboud dominate the bestseller shelves at many bookstores. More recently academics in the organizational sciences have begun to acknowledge the need for focusing research on the top management group (Hambrick & Mason 1984).

Top managers or the leaders of organizations shape and determine the behavior patterns considered acceptable in the organization. Further, the shaping of an organization is the result of the values that top management holds. Hambrick and Mason (1984) argue that organizations are a reflection of the top management or dominant coalition. They argue that the assumptions or values of top management filter and possibly distort their perceptions and interpretations of the organization and the external environment. This view is supported by March and Simon (1958) and Child (1972) who argue that leaders bring their values to bear on the activity of decision making. Child (1972, 16) notes that "constraints and opportunities are functions of the power exercised by decision-makers in the light of ideological values."

The organizational values of top management are clearly essential to an understanding of how a firm organizes but also to an understanding of the power relationships within the company. The primary designers of organizational values are the leaders or owners of a company. Chester Bernard (1938) was one of the first writers to note that executive responsibilities include the shaping of organizational values. Formulating and defining of purpose is the primary function of top management, according to Bernard in his classic book *The Functions of the Executive.*

Clark (1970) emphasized the importance of founders and strong leaders in the development of distinctive cultures. Organizational sagas (collective understandings of historical events) were found to strongly influence organizational success and loyalty, as reported in his study of American colleges (Clark 1970, 1972). Leaders who introduce and institutionalize the values of a dominant group are able to positively influence organizational participation and effectiveness. Providing a vision and rallying commitment to a purpose were discussed by Pettigrew (1979) as one of the important aspects of the leader's role. Based on his study of boarding school headmasters, Pettigrew notes that leaders personalize and strengthen their position by using symbols, language, ideologies, beliefs and myths as mechanisms to create, develop and control a culture.

According to Schein (1983), a set of shared values is "embedded" in the culture by top managers or founders. By embedding and then transmitting the basic assumptions of the organization, leaders maintain control. An organizational culture is the product of the founder's beliefs and values; hence organizational values do not emerge from scratch. The personal and work values and beliefs of a founder guide and selectively direct the development of the organization and its culture. Top management's actions emerge from their values and influence how things are done in the enterprise.

A primary activity of management is the creation of belief systems to induce compliance and commitment, according to Pfeffer (1981b). Following this perspective, managers legitimate their own power, elicit commitment, and create positive affect by constructing and maintaining systems of shared beliefs. Selznick (1957) stressed the role of leadership in the defining of mission and the maintaining of values as the tools of organizational identity and social integration beyond the formal structure.

The impact of top management on the perceptions and attitudes of all employees, from the bottom to the top, was emphasized by Ruch and Goodman (1983) in their practitioner-oriented book on top management image. They examined in detail the critical role that top management plays in establishing values. The empirical and illustrative evidence they provide supports the view that the perceptions of top management are the single most important determinant of work attitudes.

From this literature it can be concluded that top management plays a critical role in developing values. Leaders use the values they establish to create a culture and justify their own influence in the organization. In addition, the values held by top management often serve to distort or inhibit their ability to understand external threats and organizational opportunities. Departments in an organization are concerned about top management's perceptions and compete for the attention of top management.

The Men at the Top

In both of the organizations studied, the founder or chief executive officer (CEO) plays a central role in defining and directing the enterprise. Both men are driven to see their companies thrive, both have clearly articulated philosophies, and both stress the importance of the organizational image in the marketplace. The personal styles of these executives are direct and demanding. It is always clear who is in charge in these enterprises.

The founder of Food King started the company and turned it into one of the most innovative fast food organizations in the industry. For the employees at Food King, the founder is the company. According to one long time employee, all that is "good" is because of him. This leader is more than an innovator in products and marketing, he is an innovator in professionalizing and dignifying the fast food industry. Strong community commitment and openness are the most frequently acknowledged features of the CEO at Food King. Almost everyone interviewed in this organization spoke of the president with reverence and praise. He is considered kindhearted and a lamb in a sometimes brutal business. Considered a very religious man, most see him as a person they could talk to if they had a problem. The few critical words spoken about this executive during interviews with subordinates referred to his unwillingness to accept information that conflicts with what he thinks.

A written philosophy of the company identifies customers, product development, and professionalism as the central themes. An interview with the president revealed that two dominant values guide his philosophy. He believes in the employees and the desirability of company individuality. Having a strong team and being regarded as reputable in the industry are of paramount concern to him.

The CEO of Roboto is the first professional manager to control the firm. He assumed the position of president from the founder after working for the company for a brief period of time. In this high technology industry he stresses the importance of research and development to a very young and highly educated work force. He brings to the position a way of doing business that is often different from the personal styles of the young and inexperienced employees who dominate the company. Some call his way of doing business street smart; others say he is tough. Roboto is a young company in a young industry and the president expresses a sense of urgency in all of his actions. In contrast to the president of Food King, Roboto's leader is not regarded as a "nice guy," but he is viewed as confident and determined to make the enterprise a success. Employees see him as a strong and dynamic figure, yet unapproachable and preoccupied.

A written philosophy does not exist for this company, but one is being developed by the president. He has struggled with what it should say and how it should be used. During interviews he revealed that the most important values to him are servicing the customer and being a leader in the industry. He felt that one way of accomplishing these goals was to develop a unified understanding of what the company is trying to do and to get employees to believe in it. As noted earlier, the two executives did not stress the importance of profits in their interviews but later, in completing surveys, they indicated that these are important organizational values.

In this chapter a definition of organizational values has been presented. Specific types of organizational values have been identified for Roboto and Food King based on interviews with several persons and a survey of hundreds of employees. The impact of top management on the development and shaping of values was discussed and the personal characteristics of two leaders were presented. The next chapter connects the values of different subunits with those of top management to determine the importance of sharing values with top managers. Value congruity will be discussed as a facet of adopting the embedded culture and as a means of gaining attention and acquiring power.

3

Value Congruity

For those who hold them, shared values define the fundamental character of their organization, the attitude that distinguishes it from all others. In this way, they create a sense of identity for those in the organization, making employees feel special. Moreover, values are a reality in the minds of most people throughout the company, not just the senior executives.

Deal & Kennedy, *Corporate Cultures*

The popular books and articles on corporate culture strongly emphasize the importance of sharing values. Sharing and similarity are the buzz words in the practitioner arguments for value consistency and integration. Prescriptions abound calling for enhanced similarity and the integration of organizational beliefs. Clearly a key component to understanding values is acknowledging the social or shared nature of preference ordering.

In the previous chapter, organizational values were distinguished from other types of values. Emphasis was placed on the organizational culture as the context within which different preferences for actions and outcomes are established. Top managers serve the purpose of establishing and then imposing their values on others within the firm. As new employees enter the enterprise, they learn what organizational values are important to the leaders. Nevertheless, many organizational members adopt preference orderings or value priorities that are different from those of top management. Hence the possibility that some groups are in greater agreement with top management is quite likely. Although sharing is regarded as desirable, not all departments share top management's values to the same extent.

In this chapter the concept of value similarity, or more precisely value congruity, is explored. Attention is given to defining what is meant by congruity, rather than assuming a common understanding. At an empirical level the degree of value sharing within departments at Roboto and Food King is examined. Differences in value sharing across departments is also investigated. Finally, the congruity of values between departments and top management is considered. In the latter portion of the chapter two conceptualizations of congruity, perceived and latent, are defined and elaborated upon. The chapter concludes with a presentation of two approaches to the measurement of value congruity.

The Concept of Congruence

Two necessary conditions must be met for value congruity to exist in an organization. First, the same set of values must be shared by different organizational members. Similarity on organizational values, while necessary, is not sufficient. The second condition is that the set of organizational values must be regarded as important or desirable. Thus, value congruity encompasses both the sharing of values and the importance of values.* Value congruity is greater to the degree that different groups share the same important values. The greater the importance of the values, the more significance is attached to similarity. Hence, any treatment of value congruity requires similarity on important values as the diagram below illustrates.

Selection of Important Values

→ Value Congruity

Similarity of Values

As an example, let's consider the situation in which a department and top management share two sets of values, one set that is regarded as important by both parties and the other that is regarded as unimportant by at least one of the parties. The more congruent value set will be the one that is both mutually important and similar. Hence, congruity is used here to refer to both similarity and level of desirability (importance). For two different groups to be value congruent, both similarity and importance are regarded as necessary conditions.

Congruity within Departments

Blau (1967) advanced the importance of value congruity when he observed that value consensus makes social exchange possible. In the sociological literature, value consensus has been a frequently discussed topic in the context

---

*Throughout this book the terms value congruity and value similarity are used synonymously. This practice is strictly for word variety and does not suggest different meanings. Hence, value sharing and value importance are necessary components for both value similarity and value congruity.

of culture and society (Gross 1956, Parsons 1949). A commonsense approach to congruity examines the degree to which different individuals in an organization are similar in their perceptions that a particular action (means) or outcome (goal) should be valued. This approach seems reasonable and logical; however, it focuses on the individual rather than the department.

The value congruity approach advocated here stresses the common preferences of a group rather than the individual preferences of group members. This distinction is critical for understanding the process of sharing. In a review of the sociological literature on consensus, Scheff (1967) clearly distinguishes between agreement at the individual and group levels. At the group level a process occurs in which group members think everyone else agrees and this perception guides their thinking. He suggests that even when consensus does not exist, thinking that it does effects behavior in the same way that consensus would.

Adapting the research on consensus to organizational values provides the context to speculate that, within a particular department, members who think that everyone else in the department shares a particular value will behave as if the value is shared. The effect of this presumption of similarity will be reflected in behavior, even if the individual members of the department do not actually share the same values. Though perceived similarity may be quite different than actual similarity, it may profoundly affect behavior.

Similarity of organizational values within different departments was examined in Roboto and Food King. Interviewees in both companies were asked if there was a group of persons in the company whose values or preferences for running a company most closely resembled their own. Almost all of the individuals interviewed revealed that they share their preferences with others in their own department. Department members would occasionally indicate different values as being important, but always expressed the opinion that their organizational values were similar to those of others in their department. Thus the interviewees presumed similarity even when they indicated different values preferences. Newcomb (1953) argues that believing agreement exists can frequently be as critical for determining behavior as actually sharing the same orientation [value].

Two questions were asked in the company-wide surveys that addressed the degree to which respondents shared values with other members of their department. The first question asked "In general, how similar do you consider yourself to other individuals in your department in terms of what you value in the work environment?" A seven point scale ranging from very dissimilar (1) to very similar (7) was used. The average response was between slightly similar (5) and moderately similar (6) for both organizations. The second question asked, "People in my work group vary widely in their values concerning how a business should be run." Response options ranged from strongly disagree (1) to strongly agree (7). The average response for both companies was between slightly disagree (3) and a neutral response (4). Based on the responses to these two questions, departmental employees appear to regard those within their department as most value congruent.

The interview and survey questions reveal that department members see themselves as most similar to those in their own department. This finding is consistent with that of Alan Wilkins (1983) who found that employees who associate with each other tend to share common orientations that differ from the shared views of other groups. This finding is also important in that it provides support for using the department as the unit of analysis in the examining of values.

Congruity across Departments

Examination of departmental value similarity across departments was explored during the interviews. Interviewees were asked to indicate which departments were most dissimilar to theirs. Almost all interviewees found a quick response that was consistent with others in their department. For example, the operations department of one company cited the marketing department as most dissimilar. This dissimilarity was based on a "natural barrier" between these two departments regarding what they view as desirable.

Hierarchical differences did exist in responding to value similarity probes. Typically those at the bottom of the organizational hierarchy were not in a position to interact frequently with those outside of their own department. The degree of awareness of other departments' values varied with department, as well as position in the department. Generally persons in the lowest levels of the organization and those in line versus staff departments were not as knowledgeable about value similarity outside of their functional area.

Figures 3-1 and 3-2 map departmental similarity and dissimilarity for the two firms. The figures are based on probing questions regarding groups whose values resemble or do not resemble the interviewees department's values. In figure 3-1, the arrows point to departments regarded as most similar and most dissimilar in Food King. For example, the top of figure 3-1 shows the marketing department regards the finance department as most similar to its own in value preferences. In figure 3-2, the arrows point to similar and dissimilar value preferences for each department in Roboto.

To simplify the presentation, the departments were combined into groups representing areas of responsibility held by top managers. For example, operations at Food King include four regions across the company. In Roboto, engineering includes three areas of division. A check of

Figure 3-1. Value Dissimilarity and Similarity in Food King.

Departments Most Similar to Own Department

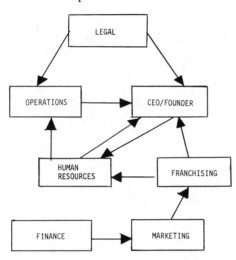

The arrow points to the department regarded as most similar to the respondent's department

Departments Most Dissimilar to Own Department

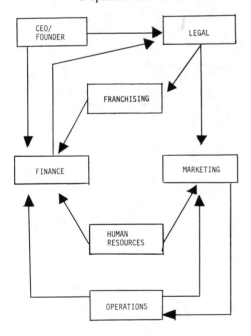

The arrow points to the department regarded as most dissimilar to the respondent's department

Figure 3-2. Value Dissimilarity and Similarity in Roboto.

Departments Most Similar to Own Department

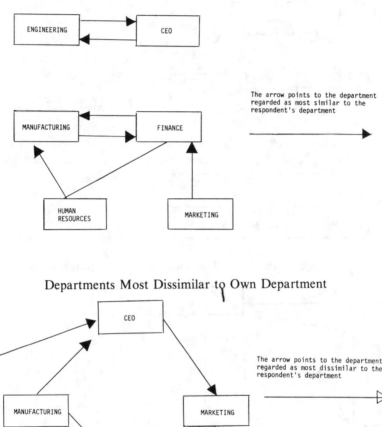

The arrow points to the department regarded as most similar to the respondent's department

Departments Most Dissimilar to Own Department

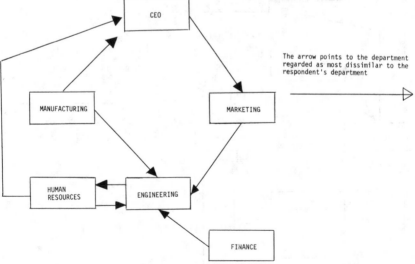

The arrow points to the department regarded as most dissimilar to the respondent's department

departmental congruity revealed that strong agreement does exist within these functional areas as noted earlier.

Examination of departmental similarity and dissimilarity of values reveals differences across organizations. In Food King, the CEO is a central figure in perceived value similarity. All the departments in this company except finance and marketing expressed similarity with the top executive. In contrast, the CEO of Roboto is viewed as sharing values in common with only one department. The department regarded as most similar to the CEO in this company is viewed as most dissimilar by every other department.

The consistency of evaluation of value similarity and dissimilarity across departments is notable. Departments do not contradict each other's assessments of value similarity, with one exception. One instance exists where a department that is viewed as most similar regards the other department as most dissimilar. This can be explained in part by the reluctance of one area head to focus on the question asked. His qualified response suggests that he was dealing with personality factors, not departmental value similarity, when responding. Department differences were noted, and value similarity with the president was strong in one company and weak in the other. Finally, respondents used their own company and department as a reference in developing their values regarding how a company should run.

One-way analyses of variance were used to discern whether individuals within departments are in greater agreement regarding their department's value congruity with top management than are individuals across departments. Table 3-1 presents the findings of these tests for each company. Three of the four tests found within department variance to be significantly smaller than between department variance. Hence, value congruity with top management is statistically different among departments in almost every case.

In summary, respondents indicated in the interviews that their values were most strongly shared by others in their department. Department members seemed to share a sense of solidarity by virtue of their common values. In addition, the analyses of variance indicated dissimilarity of values across departments. Departments assess their similarity with top management in varying degrees indicating that not all departments share the same values in common with top management.

Congruity with Top Management

To understand the importance of sharing values with top management, it is first necessary to examine the influence of values on the organizational leaders. March and Simon (1956) argued that leaders bring their own assumptions and preferences to the decision making process. The notion of strategic choice espoused by Child (1972) further supports the view of values

Table 3-1. One-Way Analysis of Variance across Departments on Perceived Value Congruity of the Most Important Value Items.

PERCEIVED VALUE CONGRUITY WITH TOP MANAGEMENT OF FOOD KING

SOURCE	SS	DF	MS	F	SIGNIFICANCE
Between Departments	31.29	13	2.41	1.556	.09
Within Departments	550.72	356	1.54		

PERCEIVED VALUE CONGRUITY WITH TOP MANAGEMENT OF ROBOTO

SOURCE	SS	DF	MS	F	SIGNIFICANCE
Between Departments	25.46	13	1.96	1.368	.21
Within Departments	54.41	38	1.43		

PERCEIVED VALUE CONGRUITY WITH THE PRESIDENT OF FOOD KING

SOURCE	SS	DF	MS	F	SIGNIFICANCE
Between Departments	36.96	13	2.84	1.833	.03
Within Departments	528.87	341	1.55		

PERCEIVED VALUE CONGRUITY WITH THE PRESIDENT OF ROBOTO

SOURCE	SS	DF	MS	F	SIGNIFICANCE
Between Departments	29.09	14	2.08	1.5643	.10
Within Departments	53.14	40	1.33		

as critical to the selection and development of strategies. As noted in chapter 2, top management brings its values to the firm and relies on these values to develop and guide the organization.

Bourgeois (1980), in a study of top management consensus on organizational goals, discovered that agreement on organizational means dramatically and positively influenced performance. Congruity on organizational means within the top management team has a positive effect on organizational functioning according to these findings. In contrast, Janis (1972) has found that group homogeneity produces inferior decisions and possibly groupthink. Whether congruity leads to functional or dysfunctional outcomes is still subject to debate. Those interested in building and changing corporate cultures suggest that value congruity is functional. Existing studies in the group literature offer qualifications on the positive outcomes stemming from consensus. Of interest in the present examination is the degree to which congruity of values exists and the effects of congruity on power relationships within the firm, regardless of whether congruity is functional or dysfunctional.

Examination of the top management teams in Roboto and Food King revealed a healthy degree of value congruity. The CEOs in both firms held organizational values that were similar to others in the executive team. The presidents stressed people issues in their discussion of their values, but did not deviate from the other executives when asked to prioritize their values.

Department-Top Management Linkages

In theory, the most important congruity relationship from the perspective of department members should be the connection between their department and top management. To the degree that a particular department is value congruent with top management, that department should be relatively more influential and have greater advantage over other departments. This argument is based on the observation that the executives' values influence strategy and thus organizational functioning. When a department shares the important values with top management, this department should be regarded by top management as being "like us" and thus worthy of trust. The more attractive the department is to top management, the greater the likelihood that department members will have access to the executive group and control over other departments. Other departments acknowledge the position of the value congruent group and the department itself operates with greater assurance and control.

There is empirical evidence that value similarity significantly influences supervisor perceptions of subordinate competency (Senger 1971). In Senger's study, subordinates with values similar to their managers' were rated higher on performance. Another study found supervisor consideration to be correlated with value similarity, and success and competency to be correlated with similarity for low self-esteem subordinates only (Weiss 1978). The limited research on value congruity offers support for the contention that similarity of values positively influences perceptions of others.

Determining Value Importance

It was noted earlier that value congruity is composed of shared values that are regarded as the most important. If departments and top managers share similar, but irrelevant organizational values, the effects of value similarity may be insignificant. Given that a measure of value congruity includes both similarity of values and degree of importance, it is necessary to refine the concept of importance.

Two interview questions investigated whether individuals separated their preferences for how a company should run from their preference for how their company should be run. Respondents did not separate their value preferences from their organizational context. That is, they discussed organizational values with their own company in mind. Throughout the interview process persons expressed the opinion that their reference point was their own department and company and that their list of values was identical to the list they would make for their company. The question "What are some of the things your company believes are important in running a company?" was answered with a list of values identical to the respondents' own list of important values or the statement "They're the same things." This indicates that the respondents' value preferences were grounded in their company experience rather than being abstractions.

Interviewees did distinguish between the rankings they assign values and the ranks the company would assign. Many felt the ranking of values would vary, the company valuing some things more than they did and vise versa. When asked if they ever worked for a company which had values that were different than their own, respondents noted they had and provided examples or descriptions to illustrate the differences.

The question of which values are most important involves the identification of a reference group. Clearly, top management is a critical group in examining values. While sharing values that top management believes to be important is essential to the measurement of value congruity, a global organizational view of importance is more appropriate if the investigation is to capture aspects of shared meanings inherent in a cultural conceptualization of organizational functioning. Determination of a subset of most important values utilized the criteria that top management should generally view the values as most important and that the departments also regard these values as critical. By incorporating the important values as indicated by both top management and all departments, the issue of importance is an organizational and shared concept, not simply a subunit or management orientation to values.

A four step procedure was followed in selecting a list of important values for Roboto and Food King. First, all respondents were asked to judge which value out of a list of twenty-four was most important for running a company. This value was ranked first. Second and third rankings were given to the second and third most important values respectively. Information provided in the previous chapter gives the frequency with which each of the values were ranked one through three for the two companies. As a second step these rankings were compared to the list of values considered most important in the interview stage of the study.

Examination of the rankings and interview data resulted in selecting six important values for Food King, including: (1) professionalism, (2) ethics, (3) efficiency, (4) superior quality and service, (5) high morale, and (6) employee development. Seven values were identified as most important in Roboto, as follows: (1) professionalism, (2) ethics, (3) industry leadership, (4) superior quality and service, (5) company growth, (6) high morale, and (7) survival.

The third and fourth stages in determining the most important values involved examining top managements' selection of the most important value and each individual department's evaluation of the most important value. A breakdown of the frequencies by department revealed a strong preference for selecting the subset of most important values. Comparison of the frequency with which top management and each individual department selected the lists of most important values provided greater confidence that representatively critical organizational values were identified for each firm.

In summary, several different approaches were taken to examining sets of value preferences within the organizations studied in order to arrive at a list of values that are most important. It is of some interest to note that the important values are not the same for Roboto and Food King and it is expected that they would be different since organizational values are developed in unique organizational cultures. Later when the relationship between value congruity and influence is explored (see chapter 4), the values utilized for examination will be only those values clearly identified as important by the bulk of organizational participants.

Perceived and Latent Value Congruity

Two distinct conceptualizations of values emerge from the literature on corporate culture. Schein (1984), for example, treats values as those aspects of the organization espoused by the dominant group. Espoused values are conscious, perceived, and explicitly articulated to serve normative or moral functions, according to this author. He goes further by distinguishing espoused values from the more tacit underlying assumptions. In contrast, Sathe (1985) uses values to mean those internalized and hard-to-change preferences. This author notes that internalized values are not easily discarded, while espoused values are more temporary.

Given the frequent use of values as espoused (Schein 1983, 1985; Deal & Kennedy 1982) or unconscious preferences (Sathe 1985, Rokeach 1968), both aspects of values will be examined. In particular, value congruity will be conceptualized in two very distinct ways. One approach to value congruity, labeled perceived value congruity, is congruity which is espoused, recognized and socially defined by a department. The other approach to value congruity, called latent value congruity, examines the underlying, unrecognized, but similar values of a department and top management. These two ways of examining value congruity will be considered separately because of their possible distinctiveness.

Perceived Value Congruity

Perceived value congruity is used here to refer to similarity of values that are consciously recognized by a department. Department members must be mindful of the values of top management in order to make comparisons and espouse similarity. They may not know what top management believes and usually do not know, but they must form some impression of top management's values in order to make the comparisons.

In addition, this view of congruity is highly subjective in that the determination of congruity is dependent on the social context of the department. For example, a department may consider itself to be very similar to top management, while top management and others do not share this perception. A discrepancy may exist between "actual" value congruity and what a department perceives as value congruity. The importance of perceived value congruity, whether or not the values are truly shared, is that the department acts on what it perceives. This approach relies on believing congruity exists and highlights the importance of the social construction of reality.

Latent Value Congruity

A different approach to value congruity, called latent value congruity, does not require awareness of the similarity of values or knowledge of the comparison group. Latent value congruity is a term used here to refer to similar values of which the groups are not directly aware. This form of value congruity can be derived by comparing the value preferences of various groups with those of top management and then calculating statistically the degree of similarity. Using this approach, department members do not make the comparison of values. Department members are not actively mindful of the value similarity between their department and top management, and do not need to believe that similarity exists. Both groups' value sets are compared, but neither group is directly aware of value similarity.

It is easy to see how these two approaches to congruity could yield very different findings. For example, department A may perceive that it has values which differ from top management, but examination of department A's values apart from the perceptions reveals similarity of values. Both approaches are considered desirable in an investigation of value congruity because they have the potential of capturing different aspects of value similarity.

Distinguishing between Perceived and Latent Value Congruity

Perceived and latent value congruity are qualitatively different indicators of shared values. Perceived value congruity may have multiple motivational bases, while latent value congruity lacks a formulated motive. For example, perceived value congruity may, following the schemes of Etzioni (1961) and Kelman (1958, 1974), be calculated for department gain, be morally derived, or the result of identification with top managers. If espoused value congruity is motivated by compliance or political gain, then departmentally perceived congruity will not match latent congruity. In contrast, if espoused congruity is motivated by identification or internalization, then analyzing both perceived and latent value congruity should yield similar findings. Regardless of the specific motives behind expressed similarity, intentionality is a necessary component.

Latent value congruity is unexpressed or unintended similarity. Department members do not attempt to speculate on top management's values; they merely express their own organizationally related values. The congruity of latent values is a realized similarity, not an intended or desired similarity. This level of value similarity should be less forced than espoused value congruity. Latent value congruity may capture identification with top management or morally derived similarity to a greater extent than perceived value congruity, because no attempt is made to consciously explicate similarity. Perceived value congruity may address a more contrived or fabricated similarity based on image control or ingratiation. Which is closer to "actual" value congruity may be impossible and even meaningless to determine.

The advantage of exploring these two approaches to value congruity is that they may reveal different aspects of similarity. The degree to which perceived and latent value congruity are associated is of interest in trying to understand how value congruity operates in organizations. In the next section of this chapter, instruments for the measurement of value congruity will be presented.

Measuring Perceived Value Congruity

When department members evaluate the degree of similarity between their department's values and those of top management, they are consciously assessing the degree of value congruity. Perceptual congruity emphasizes the individual's definition of similarity. A measure of perceived value congruity was developed that focuses on department members' views of similarity of values (Enz 1985a). This instrument, presented in appendix C, asks respondents to indicate the degree of similarity on twenty-four value statements between their department and the president and their department and top management excluding the president. A seven-point scale is used, ranging from very dissimilar to very similar. A "don't know" choice is also available.

This measure of value congruity examines congruity with both the CEO and the entire management team. Two separate reference groups were developed as a result of comments made during the interviews at Roboto and Food King. Employees regarded value congruity with the president to be distinct from value congruity with the other members of the top management team. Hence, the congruity measure focuses on top management and the president individually. The responses of each department member to the twenty-four value statements were summed to arrive at a total similarity score for each individual. Individual scores are aggregated to the department level to provide a composite mean score for each department on these two categories of congruity.

During the interview stage of the study, the twenty-four value statements were isolated from a larger list because of their perceived importance. While all twenty-four value statements were deemed important values, some value statements were ranked as stronger preferences and thus deemed more important than others. Importance was determined by examining the frequency with which subjects ranked a value as most important in the survey. These rankings were compared with the list of most important values gathered through open-ended questions and the card sort during the interview stage of the study. Separate lists were developed for the two companies.

A subgroup of these important values was identified (following the procedure elaborated on earlier in this chapter) and used to refine the measure of perceived value congruity. By summing only the value statements regarded as most important in the two stages of the study, unique value similarity measures were obtained for Roboto and Food King. Mean similarity scores were obtained for each individual department member and were aggregated to provide a composite mean score for each department.

Two orientations were identified, one stressing congruity with top management as a team, the other concentrating on congruity with the CEO exclusively. An overall measure of congruity was developed using a complete list of values and another measure using a subset of values. In sum, a total of four different measures of perceived value congruity were devised for the investigation into the role of value congruity in determining departmental influence.

Value similarity from the perspective of top management is also examined. A special one-page survey was mailed to all top managers in the two companies. This instrument asked top managers, including the presidents, to indicate the degree of similarity between top management (including themselves) and each department in the organization on each of the most important values and an overall question of value similarity. A seven-point scale ranging from very dissimilar to very similar was used. A "don't know" option was also provided. The results of this instrument are two measures of value similarity from the viewpoint of top managers. One measure focuses on similarity of the most important value statements, while the other measure is a general indicator of similarity. The top managers' scores are aggregated to provide composite measures.

Measuring Latent Value Congruity

To measure the degree of unrecognized congruity between a department's values and those of top management, frequency distributions were developed for each department and top management on the rankings of the value items. Department frequency distributions (X_i) are compared with the frequency distributions for top management (Y_j) to obtain an index of net difference (ND_{xy}). Subtracting the index of net difference from one constitutes a measure of the similarity of value statements or value congruity.

The index of net difference was developed by Stanley Lieberson (1976) and is a variation on the Wilcoxon-rank sum statistic (see Hollander & Wolfe 1973). The purpose of the index is to give the difference between two probabilities of inequality. The index was selected for this study of latent value congruity because the index can be used in comparisons where the variable of interest is skewed within each group (department), comparisons are made in terms of some ordered characteristics (rank), and the order of the characteristic may be different in each group (Lieberson 1976). The index of net difference also takes into account ties, while the Mann-Whitney U test and Deuchler's approach do not (Lieberson 1976, Hollander & Wolfe 1972).

Finally the Wilcoxon-type rank sum statistics focus on the test of significance rather than describing the magnitude and direction of differences between groups.

To calculate the index of net difference three comparisons between departments and top management are needed. The three comparisons include: the probability that X (any department's frequency) will exceed Y (top management's frequency) with respect to I (value statements), $\text{pr}(X > Y)$; the probability that Y will exceed X, $\text{pr}(Y > X)$; and the probability that X and Y will be equal, $\text{pr}(X = Y)$. These three probabilities sum to unity $[\text{pr}(X=Y) + \text{pr}(X>Y) + \text{pr}(Y>X) = 1.0]$. The index will be zero if the two probabilities of inequality are equal $[\text{pr}(X = Y)]$; in this case a net difference does not exist. When considerable overlap exists between the distribution of a department and top management, the index of net difference will reflect this. For example, if $\text{pr}(X = Y)$ is .75, the maximum net difference score would be .25 $[\text{pr}(X \neq Y)]$. The index and the measure of congruity are obtained using the following formula:

$$ND_{xy} = \text{pr}(X > Y) - \text{pr}(Y > X)$$

Measure of net similarity $= 1 - ND_{xy}$

$$\text{where,} \quad \text{pr}(X > Y) = \sum_{i=2}^{n} X_i \left(\sum_{j=1}^{n=i-1} Y_j \right)$$

$$\text{pr}(Y > X) = \sum_{i=2}^{n} Y_i \left(\sum_{j=1}^{n=i-1} X_j \right)$$

Although the index of net difference provides statements concerning directionality, the present study will not be concerned with directionality. It is not of interest here which group possesses more or less similarity, but rather the absolute net difference. Ordinal data (value ranks) were collected to measure latent value congruity; however, the calculation of a net difference score ranging from values of 0 to 1 constitutes a measurement scale transformation. The difference score is a probabilistic measure which allows for measurement intervals with arithmetic values. While the data collected was ordinal in nature, the comparison of the data utilized an index with equal intervals and a true zero. Analysis of latent value congruity is based on the index making it appropriate to treat the measurement statistic (the net difference score) as a ratio scale measure. Given that a ratio scale measure of latent value congruity exists, a parametric approach to data analysis is merited.

A measure of net similarity is acquired by subtracting the index of net difference from one $[1 - ND_{xy} = \text{Net Similarity}]$. Four different similarity scores are calculated for each department in this study. First a similarity score was obtained for each department comparing the frequencies of the twenty-four value statements ranked number one by each department and top management. A second score compared the frequencies of all values ranked number two. A selective list of most important value statements was used to develop additional net difference indexes. Using a list of most important values (identical to the list used in measuring perceived congruity) two additional scores were developed comparing the frequencies of important values ranked #1 and #2 by each department and top management.

In summary, four measures of latent value congruity were computed. The first two measures involved comparisons of the frequencies of response on all value statements ranked first and second by departments and top management. The second measures restrict frequency comparisons to the value statements felt to be most important to the running of an organization. These measures are exploratory and are developed to determine whether subsets of important values affect the perceptions of power associated with value congruity.

Summary

This chapter has attempted to clarify what value congruity is and why it is important to consider congruity between functional departments and top management. In addition, congruity was broken down into two forms, perceived and latent. Depending on the form of congruity examined, it is likely that different relationships with departmental influence will exist. Finally, this chapter provided a description of several measures developed to examine value congruity.

Taking this chapter together with chapter 2, the stage has been set for an empirical test of the relationship between value congruity and departmental power. In the next chapter we will return to the theoretical development presented in chapter 1 and we will review the findings of a study that examined value congruity as a determinant of departmental power. In addition, the next chapter explores the incremental variation in departmental power uniquely associated with value congruity when critical contingency factors are present. Finally, chapter 4 explores the strength of the relationship between the two forms of value congruity and department power in an attempt to ascertain whether perceived or latent value congruity has a stronger relationship with power.

4

Values: The Key to Power

In a recent editorial, a *Washington Post* columnist commented on the Reagan administration noting that the president is a "living refutation" to the phrase "knowledge is power" (Broder 1985). The columnist went on to argue that Ronald Reagan has clearly demonstrated that "conviction is power." The writer was critical of the president for his adherence to ideology in the face of contrary information, but he missed the more global implication that all chief executives operate on beliefs as well as facts. Each decision or choice a top executive makes is made in terms of his or her organizationally defined values. Values are deep seated and may even be unconscious; hence, their influence on our behavior may be overlooked.

Within the political sphere, criticism is also directed at subordinates who parrot executive views and refuse to rock the boat. Using a value congruity explanation, the actions of subordinates appear to be prudent, although possibly dysfunctional. If executives find it necessary to make decisions based on values, it seems likely that subordinate groups will gain and maintain power to the extent that they share and/or reinforce these values. A few examples serve to illustrate the connection between values and power.

A small solar energy company recently went through a reorganization, and one department lost most of its responsibility for critical activities. Interestingly the department continued to wield power by virtue of the strong connection between this functional group and the president (Nuttall 1985).

The company president of a small manufacturing firm views himself as religious and has hired many Christians who believe as he does. The CEO has placed the company under God's will. In this organization, those who value what top management values are apt to gain power. How does a department acquire additional power in this organization? Clearly, controlling critical uncertainties alone is not enough. Does a department that fails to control resources lose power? Probably not if they simply argue that their inability to control uncertainties is "God's will."

These examples highlight the important connection between value congruity and departmental influence. It was argued in chapter 1 that value congruity will serve as a useful determinant of power. This view is in contrast to the explanation based on control of critical resources also discussed in the first chapter. Numerous anecdotes and examples can be raised to provide support for the contention that values and power are inextricably linked in organizational functioning. However, a stronger body of support is necessary to verify the degree to which value congruity explains departmental power.

In order to validate the contention that organizational value sharing and power are associated, this chapter will provide qualitative and quantitative data from a study of two medium-sized organizations. Three specific questions will be addressed. First, is there a strong relationship between value congruity and departmental power? Second, is value congruity a useful additional explanation of department power beyond the explanation provided by the critical contingencies models? Finally, what is the connection between latent or unrecognized value similarity and perceived value congruity as they relate to departmental power? Those interested in the specific research hypotheses that correspond to these questions should refer to appendix D.

Power Differences

Before examining the linkage between departmental power and value similarity, it is essential to determine whether power differences among departments are present and also whether individuals within the same department agree on the nature of their department's power. To explore these questions requires a quantitative analysis of power differences in Roboto and Food King.

The purpose behind this analysis is to discern whether individuals within departments are in greater agreement regarding their own department's power than are individuals across departments. The interviews in Roboto and Food King indicated that employees express the greatest degree of similarity with those in their own department when evaluating the power of different subunits. Using analysis of variance is a quantitative way to test within department agreement and also to determine if power differences are present across departments.

Examination of power differences required investigating the two companies separately using several one-way analyses of variance. Failure to find differences would suggest: (1) departments do not significantly differ in their levels of power, or (2) the measures used are not sensitive indicators of the power construct, or (3) heterogeneity of variance masks significant differences. The summary presented in table 4-1 shows that a significant difference exists among departments for both companies. This finding is essential to insure that departmental power is meaningfully distinguished across departments, and that agreement exists among department members.

Table 4-1. One-Way Analysis of Variance across Departments on Issue-Oriented Departmental Power.

SOURCE	ISSUE-ORIENTED DEPARTMENTAL POWER Food King				
	SS	DF	MS	F	SIGNIFICANCE
Between Departments	2613.04	13	201.33	2.515	.0027
Within Departments	26777.48	335	79.93		

SOURCE	ISSUE-ORIENTED DEPARTMENTAL POWER Roboto				
	SS	DF	MS	F	SIGNIFICANCE
Between Departments	1907.61	14	136.26	2.717	.0073
Within Departments	1905.67	38	50.15		

Knowing that power differences exist among departments and that persons in the same department view power similarly allows us to continue exploring departmental power at the subunit level of analysis. If individuals in the same department differed dramatically on how they examined departmental power, aggregation of individual perceptions to represent a collective departmental perspective would be misleading. Fortunately, individuals in the same department appear to agree to a much greater degree than do individuals in different departments.

Facets of Power

Any attempt to examine organizational power requires serious consideration of two questions. First, whose perceptions of power matter in evaluating intraorganizational power? It is insufficient to rely exclusively on the collective perceptions of department members regarding their department's power. The opinions of top management and other departments are also necessary, and occasionally more critical. Secondly, what is the best way to measure a department's power? Is power situation specific or an overall global ability to effect outcomes? Because a variety of opinions exist regarding the most suitable means for measuring power and the critical evaluating group, several different perspectives and measures of power are utilized in this book.

Multiple Perspectives

Whose opinion matters in determining department power? In this study, perceptions of power are examined from the perspective of: (1) each department's appraisal of their own power, (2) other departments' appraisal of each department's power, and (3) top management's appraisal of each department's power. This multiple approach to power is adopted to avoid common method bias, and ascertain the degree of consistency that different groups have concerning departmental power. Clegg (1975) observes that most research on departmental power relies on department heads to represent the views of the department. By using multiple respondents, the criticism of managerial bias is eliminated.

Although it is expected that value congruity will be associated with power regardless of who evaluates a department's power, it cannot be assumed a priori that different groups have comparable perceptions. Existing literature suggests that departments often overrate their own power, and are more accurate in their perceptions of other departments' power (Hinings et al. 1974). Similarly, if top management does not see the department as powerful, the probability that the department will exert influence is reduced. Hence, the frame of reference of the perceiving group can be critical in understanding power.

Multiple Measures

Different aspects of departmental power are captured by examining overall power versus issue-specific power (Enz 1985c). A general measure of power attempts to capture the overall influence of each department. Issue-specific power represents power in various situations or contexts (see appendix A for a discussion of these measures). Previous work on power has concentrated on either general or issue-oriented power, but not both.

The need to use multiple measures of power arises from the possibility that general and issue-oriented power may be tapping different components of power. For example, it is possible that general power examines the potential to influence, while issue-specific power reflects the exercise of power in specific situations.

In sum, the use of multiple comparison groups and multiple measures allows for the determination of the convergent and discriminant validity of power. Collecting perceptions from three different groups on two different measures allows for examining the presence or absence of across group differences and measurement consensus.

Linking Value Congruity with Power

What is the nature of the relationship between value congruity and power? It was suggested in chapter 1 that departments that agreed with top management on organizational values would be perceived as powerful. The preliminary interviews and contact with personnel in Roboto and Food King served the purpose of qualitatively determining which departments were regarded as most and least powerful.

Determining Powerful Departments

The departments identified frequently as being most or least powerful are noted in table 4-2. Figures 4-1 and 4-2 map the departments considered most and least able to affect outcomes as viewed by top managers. The arrows in these figures point to departments regarded as most and least powerful. By comparing the responses of all interviewees (see table 4-2) with the mapped responses of top management, a strong degree of agreement is evident. Once again the views of department heads are supported by the responses of departmental members.

Departments identified as most powerful in the interviews were also considered to share similar values with other departments and top executives. Referring back to figures 3-1 and 3-2 in the previous chapter and comparing departmental similarity to the departments identified as powerful provides visual demonstration of the connection between similarity of values and departmental power. For example, the CEO in Roboto selected only one department as most similar in values, and this department was also considered by 74.0% of the respondents to be powerful and by all of the top management team. In Food King the relationship between perceived power and value similarity is not as clear. Finance, for example, was considered most powerful by some (31.8%) and least powerful by others (16.7%).

Two findings come out of the qualitative investigation of power. First, power differences associated with departments are easy to identify. Second, for Food King, there is some degree of inconsistency in linking power with value congruity, while Roboto provides strong evidence to suggest that value similarity with the president is related to power. The results of the interviews suggest that similarity of values and power are intertwined. The nature of the link is clearly recognized at Roboto and less consistently identified in Food King.

Table 4-2. Frequency of Response:
Most and Least Powerful Departments and/or Functional Areas.[+]

Food King

DEPARTMENTS	FREQUENCY OF RESPONSE*			
	Most Powerful (n=44)		Least Powerful (n=42)	
	%	(n)	%	(n)
Marketing	52.3%	(23)	0.0%	(0)
Corp. Operations	45.5%	(20)	2.4%	(1)
Finance	31.8%	(14)	16.7%	(7)
Human Resources (Personnel)	20.5%	(9)	2.4%	(1)
Franchising	18.2%	(8)	0.0%	(0)
Top Management	15.9%	(7)	2.4%	(1)
Development	9.1%	(4)	9.5%	(4)
Purchasing	9.1%	(4)	4.8%	(2)
Regional Operations	9.1%	(4)	0.0%	(0)
Stores	2.3%	(1)	16.7%	(7)
Training	0.0%	(0)	2.4%	(1)
Legal	0.0%	(0)	28.6%	(12)

Roboto

DEPARTMENTS	FREQUENCY OF RESPONSE			
	Most Powerful (n=23)		Least Powerful (n=17)	
	%	(n)	%	(n)
Engineering	74.0%	(17)	0.0%	(0)
Marketing	48.0%	(11)	0.0%	(0)
Top Management	22.0%	(5)	0.0%	(0)
Finance	8.7%	(2)	53.0%	(9)
Manufacturing	4.3%	(1)	41.2%	(7)
Human Resources (Personnel)	0.0%	(0)	70.6%	(12)

[+]This set of departments is a reduced list which represents functional areas under the control of vice presidents.
*The responses are multiple ones and therefore will not total 100%.

A Department's Perspective on Values

Surveys distributed to the employees at Roboto and Food King were used to explore quantitatively the relationship between perceived value congruity and power. Department members were asked to evaluate: (1) the similarity between their department and top management, and (2) the similarity between their department and the president on organizational values (see appendix C for the instrument used to measure perceived value congruity). These indicators of a department's value congruity were correlated with several different evaluations of the department's power. As noted earlier, the evaluation of a department's power was provided by the department, other departments, and top management. Hence, the purpose of this portion of the study was to examine the linkages between the following:

```
Department's Perceived Value Congruity     AND     The Evaluation of Power
                                                   (General and Issue Power)

                                              →    The Department
   with Top Management              ═══════════→    Other Departments
                                              →    Top Management

Department's Perceived Value Congruity     AND     The Evaluation of Power
                                                   (General and Issue Power)

                                              →    The Department
   with the President               ═══════════→    Other Departments
                                              →    Top Management
```

Pearson product-moment correlation coefficients were utilized to test the relationship between perceived value congruity and the three orientations toward department power. This statistic provides an indication of the magnitude and the direction of the relationships (Kerlinger 1975). The coefficient is a standard measure of linear relationship and is independent of a unit of measurement.

It is argued that if a department perceives itself to share similar values with top management and the president, that subunit will be thought of as powerful. Congruity with top management excluding the president was separated from congruity with the president because the interviews revealed employees in both companies distinguished between the president and other top managers when discussing value similarity issues.

Congruity with top management and the president was significantly related to department power as perceived by the department and top management. The results presented in table 4-3 suggest that the stronger correlations between value congruity and power are evident when the department evaluates its own similarity and influence. A department sees itself as more powerful when it is more value congruent with top management and/or the president.

In contrast, other departments' evaluations of a department's power are not associated with value congruity as seen by the department. Hence, if a department sees itself as value similar with top management, this perception has no relationship with how other departments see the department's influence.

Top management's evaluation of a department's power is associated with

Figure 4-1. Most and Least Powerful Departments in Food King.

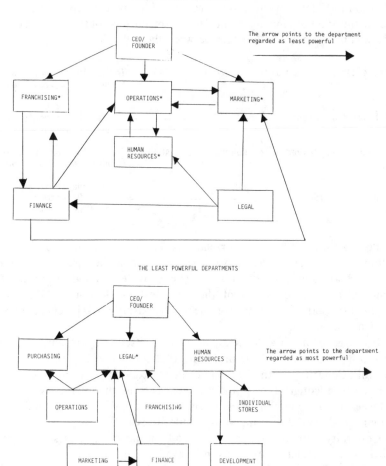

*These departments consider their own department to be powerful/powerless.

the department's perceived value congruity with top management. Power, as evaluated by the top management team, is not as strongly associated with a department's congruity with the president. Hence, departments who see themselves as congruent with top management are regarded as powerful by top management. Departmental similarity with the president does not yield the same correlation with top management's assessment of the subunit's power. If the president is less involved or dominant in the day to day activities of the firm, it makes sense that top management would not make a strong connection between department power and value congruity with the CEO.

Figure 4-2. Most and Least Powerful Departments in Roboto.

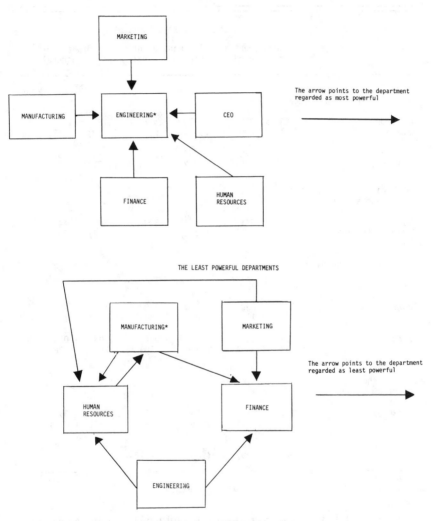

*These departments consider their own department to be powerful/powerless.

Two forms of power were examined: general and issue specific power. Of the two facets of power, the general assessment of influence represented a stronger correlation with value congruity than the issue specific influence variable. This finding indicates that a non-reference specific indicator of power is more highly associated with values than is a concrete multiple context indicator. Clearly, an overall measure of power captures the potential

Table 4-3.   Pearson Product-Moment Correlations between Value
Congruity and Departmental Power.

| | Perceptual Measures of Power | | | | | |
| | Own Department | | Top Management | | Other Departments | |
	Issues	General	Issues	General	Issues	General
Departmental Perspective						
Perceived Value Congruity						
With Top	.385	.718	.310	.466	.187	.403
Management	(.021)	(.0001)	(.054)	(.006)	(.170)	(.017)
With the	.512	.378	.292	.243	.090	.193
President	(.002)	(.022)	(.062)	(.102)	(.321)	(.158)
Top Management Perspective						
Perceived Value Congruity						
With	.376	.341	.354	.539	.308	.442
Departments	(.022)	(.035)	(.030)	(.001)	(.052)	(.008)
Latent Value Congruity						
On All Values						
Ranked #1	-.408	.230	.030	.210	.198	.239
	(.014)	(.116)	(.439)	(.139)	(.152)	(.106)
Ranked #2	.236	-.084	.032	-.044	.103	-.056
	(.108)	(.333)	(.434)	(.410)	(.297)	(.386)
On Only the						
Important Values						
Ranked #1	.129	.215	.289	.334	.286	.337
	(.252)	(.131)	(.064)	(.038)	(.067)	(.037)
Ranked #2	.134	.051	.098	.045	.094	.094
	(.249)	(.398)	(.309)	(.410)	(.317)	(.318)

Note: The significance levels are presented in parentheses in terms of p values.

to influence while the issue measure stresses influence situations or events. Values may be more clearly attached to the potential to influence than the actual instance of influencing.

The findings reported here also suggest that value similarity and power are more strongly linked when the evaluators of power are the department or top management. Third parties such as other departments are not persuaded to evaluate a department as powerful simply because the department sees itself as value congruent with top management.

Other departments may not see another department's power as being linked to congruity because they do not have sufficient information to judge the department's ability to affect outcomes (issue based power). This would explain why a general measure of other departments' perceptions of power was found to be associated with congruity but the issue-oriented measure was insignificant. Other departments are removed from the interaction between a department and top management and even further removed from the interaction between a department and the president. As a third party, other departments may have very little information to use in assessing power. When asked about other departments during the interviews, many persons found it easy to assess general power but confessed that they knew little information about how other departments influenced key issues.

Intradepartmental conflict (Bacharach & Lawler 1980) is another factor that may affect how departments evaluate other departments' power. The mixed motives behind evaluating another department's power may lead to under-evaluations of power. The literature suggests that departments tend to over evaluate their own power (Hinings et al. 1974). It is possible that departments will under evaluate other departments' power because they compete for top management attention and influence. This motive may explain the insignificant findings.

In sum, if departments believe they share values in common with the top managers, they perceive themselves as powerful and are perceived as powerful by top management. The degree of association is greatest between a department's own power perceptions and their value congruity with the organizational leaders. A general measure of power is more strongly associated with value congruity than the measure of power based on specific power issues. Finally, top management's views of power are more strongly related to congruity with top management than to congruity with the president.

These findings lend support to the literature which argues that shared values, as one aspect of culture, influence perceptions of organizational functioning. Given the inherent conflict between departments, the tendency for departments to overvalue their own power in the organization, and the possibility of other departments' undervaluing a department's power, the perceptions of top management are perhaps the most critical in understanding the value congruity/power link.

Top Management's Perspective on Values

Departmental similarity of values with top management may be quite different depending on whether the congruity is in the minds of department members or top managers. Given the possible differences in perceptions, value congruity is investigated from the perspective of the top managers as a group.

It is argued that the greater the degree to which top management perceives a department to be similar to itself on organizational values, the more powerful the department should be. The logic of this argument is that if the executives believe a department to be value congruent, then others in the organization should regard the department as powerful.

To determine the connection between value congruity as assessed by top management and departmental power, quantitative data were collected from Food King and Roboto. The findings reported in table 4-3 reveal very strong relationships between perceived value congruity and power. From the data presented, it is clear that departmental power as perceived by a department, top management, and other departments, is significantly related to top management's perceptions of value congruity. Thus, value congruity as determined by top management, and the three different perspectives on departmental power are all significantly related. When top management believes itself to be similar to a department on a set of values, every group in the firm sees the value similar department as powerful.

The literature on top management image (Ruck & Goodman 1983) argues that the views of executives significantly shape the attitudes of other organizational members. In this study other departments' perceptions of a department's power were associated with top management's perceptions of value congruity. This finding is particularly interesting in light of the lack of support for the value congruity/power linkage when the department versus top management was assessing value congruity. Other departments' perceptions of a department's power are associated with value congruity only when congruity is perceived by top management. It appears that other departments are more aware of or in agreement with the perceptions of top management. Departments may be in tune with top management's perceptions to a greater degree than they are with the views of other departments. Empire building, image management, or simply top management clout are possible explanations for why other departments' evaluations of a department's power are significantly associated with congruity as viewed by executives.

Top management's perceptions of congruity may be the most relevant in determining how subunits perceive departmental power. If top managers allocate resources and design the culture, it is plausible that departments are powerful when they are perceived as sharing similar values by top management.

In general, stronger association exists between general power and perceived value congruity than between issue-oriented power and congruity. The differences in the magnitude of the power/values relationships may be attributable to the aspects of power that the two measures are capturing. The general measure may be tapping the intangible facets of power, while the issue measure explicates the reference point for evaluating power. Given the intangible nature of shared values, congruity may be tied to a general, overriding notion of power. This would explain why value sharing and general power are more strongly associated than issue power and values. Many respondents in the interviews felt that issue related power addressed functional responsibility or the right to influence, as opposed to the ability to influence. Hence, the general measure of power may be revealing the informal aspects of influence to a much greater extent than the issue measure of power.

Taken together, the results indicate consistently that top management's perceptions of value congruity are related to departmental power, regardless of the organizational unit appraising a particular department's power. Further, these findings constitute the first empirical support for the importance of value congruity in determining power. The results of this portion of the study build on the value similarity literature (Senger 1971, Weiss 1978) and offer support at the departmental level.

Latent Value Congruity and Perceptions of Power

The discussion of power and value congruity presented in the first portion of this chapter has concentrated on congruity as perceived by top management or department members. These aspects of value congruity stress conscious evaluation or espoused similarity. Because it is possible for a subunit to express similarity, but not select the same value preferences as another group, unconscious similarity of values will also be examined. Shifting to latent value congruity requires examining values that are not explicitly regarded as similar, but are matched between two groups. Hence, latent value congruity captures the unconscious or calculated similarity between organizational departments and top management. By matching the values of different groups similarity can be determined.

Using the four latent measures of value congruity presented in chapter 3, the linkage between power and value similarity was examined. It is argued that departments sharing values in common with top management, even though both parties are unaware of the similarity, will be perceived as powerful by other departments, top management, and themselves.

Table 4-3 presents the product-moment correlations between various components of latent value congruity and perceptions of power. The results indicate weak findings regarding the latent congruity measures. Only five of the twenty-four measures of latent congruity were significantly related to perceptions of power ($p < .10$).

Four of the five significant relationships involved only the most important values, and further restricted the measurement of similarity to those values ranked as the most important (#1). Both top management and other departments' evaluations of a department's power were positively related to latent value congruity. While these correlations were not large, they were significant. Congruent values ranked second are of no importance in the linkage with power, indicating that power is only associated with unconscious similarity on the most important values. Hence, top management and other departments' evaluations of a department's power are only weakly associated with the latent value similarity between the department and top management.

Interestingly, when a department evaluates its own power, the relationship between power and latent value congruity was not significant, with one exception. The only significant linkage between congruity and power is somewhat surprising. A strong negative relationship was found to exist between latent value congruity on the values identified in the interviews and a department's evaluation of its own power. In other words, the department regarded itself as less powerful if latent value congruity was strong. Unlike top management and other departments, department members did not evaluate their own department as powerful when their departmental values were congruent with top management.

The most striking results of this analysis are the differences in the relationships between the various groups' (i.e. departments, top management, and other departments) perceptions of power and the unconscious measures of value similarity. For top management and other departments, the greater the degree of unrecognized similarity on the most important values, the greater their evaluations of a department's power. The significant but negative correlation between a department's perception of its own power and latent congruity is contrary to the anticipated relationship. The unusual negative relationship between latent value congruity and power for a department may reveal the complexities of perceived versus latent value congruity.

Perceived and latent value congruity may be tapping very different aspects of value congruity. As noted earlier, perceived congruity may be based on the espoused or organizationally formulated values. The bulk of the culture literature deals with the values that the companies teach organizational participants. These values fall into the category of perceived or espoused. As several researchers have noted, these are the values which management presents to legitimate their actions (Kamens 1977), indoctrinate newcomers (Van Maanen & Schein 1979), or induce compliance and commitment (Pfeffer 1981b). Cultural control and manipulation of organizational involvement may be the objectives of top managers' efforts in attaining congruity on these perceived or consciously articulated values.

Departmental employees, through the process of socialization or because of their organizational savvy, may express similarity. Values do not need to be similar (latent congruity) so long as they are perceived to be similar. Following the logic of W.I. Thomas, if department members believe their department is similar to top management, it is similar. Weick (1969, 135) captures this idea by noting "believing is seeing." Departments may identify with top management and believe they are similar. In this case it does not matter that they are dissimilar; they function as if they are similar.

A motive based explanation would suggest that consciously perceived similarity of values by a department may be used instrumentally to gain power or advantage. In this instance, departments may be aware of their differences but choose to express similarity.

Because latent value congruity is unconscious and a calculated measure of similarity, it may be measuring intrinsic values rather than values constructed to control behavior and create positive effect. Powerful departments maintain their power by knowing when and how to express similarity; that does not mean that they actually share the values of top management. It is very likely that top management values things that the rest of the organization does not realize, either because departments lack information or because executives are skilled at creating an image that is incongruent with their "actual" beliefs.

For example, in one company studied, many persons expressed the opinion that top management valued the team spirit and "family feeling" above all else. In contrast, the top managers reflected on the importance of valuing the stockholders and growth in sales. When asked how they felt about the team concept, they remarked that it was important for employees to identify with this concept. In other interviews departmental employees would qualify a response by saying, "The president would want me to say . . . ." These interviewees suggested that they knew what the company thinks should be valued (the party line), and they knew how to parrot back these values.

From the perspective of departments, those who are politically sophisticated may manage their image while keeping their own set of preferences for running a business separate and intact. In this case, a difference exists between latent and perceived values. When latent values and perceived values are consistent, it is possible that expressed similarity is not guided by instrumental motives, but is genuine.

Interestingly, top management's and other departments' perceptions of a department's power are positively related to latent congruity. If a department shares the latent (unconscious) values for running a business with top management, they are powerful. The inconsistency between perceived and latent congruity is not present for top management. One possible explanation for this finding is that a greater degree of consistency exists between perceived congruity and latent congruity for top managers. Top management has fewer reasons to knowingly express similarity with a department that differs from the unconsciously shared values.

To explain the contrast in findings for departments and top management, it is necessary to examine the relationship between perceived and latent value congruity. If these measures of value similarity are consistent—that is, perceived and latent congruity are positively related—then both measures of similarity should be positively associated with power. This would explain the positive relationships between latent congruity and power for top managers. Examination of what may be a value gap (difference) between perceived and latent values may explain the findings for departments. A gap is present when a negative relationship exists between perceived value congruity and latent value congruity. The negative relationship between latent congruity and power for a department may be attributable to a value gap between the perceived and unconscious facets of similarity. The gap between these two facets of congruity will be discussed in detail later in this chapter.

Critical Contingencies and Departmental Power

The previous section summarized data that showed a significant relationship to exist between value congruity and departmental power. What remains to be investigated is the robustness of the relationship. In other words, is value congruity a useful supplemental determinant of power? Given the existing literature that suggests control of critical contingencies determines power, the data reported in this section will examine the unique variance in power explained by value congruity, taking into consideration the critical contingencies variables. Hence, the second research question examines whether any additional variation in departmental power can be uniquely explained by value congruity.

As noted in chapter 1, critical contingencies explanations dominate common interpretations of departmental power. According to these models, the department most capable of controlling environmental uncertainties or critical problems will be regarded as the most powerful. The argument set forth in this book is that value congruity also determines which departments are regarded as most powerful. The focus of this second research question is to ascertain whether value congruity provides an explanation of power beyond the explanation provided by critical contingencies.

Figure 4-3 provides a model of power that incorporates both value congruity and critical contingencies perspectives. This model introduces value congruity as a supplemental explanatory factor in a critical contingencies model of power. The external and internal environments of an organization are considered to be sources of values, as well as sources of unknowns. The approach advanced here is that departmental power is determined by the interplay of a subunit's congruity of values with top management, and its ability to control critical uncertainties. Exclusive attention to a critical contingencies explanation of power is restrictive; hence, the development of a model to incorporate values as an additional determinant of power. Values, according to this model, continue to operate after departments attain power as a means of legitimating and perpetuating existing power. The feedback loops in figure 4-3 illustrate the process of legitimation and show how specific values and definitions of critical contingencies are perpetuated over time; thus, the powerful stay powerful.

To investigate the question of whether value congruity provides any additional explanation of power a hierarchical multiple regression analysis is needed. A hierarchical procedure allows for a unique partitioning of total variance in department power (Cohen & Cohen 1975). The order of entry of the independent variables is determined a priori by the purpose of this research. The critical contingencies variable is entered first, followed by the value congruity measure. After entering the value congruity variable it is possible to determine the increase in departmental power accounted for by value congruity when the previously entered critical contingencies variable has been partialled out. Figure 4-4 provides a visual presentation of the variance in departmental power explained by the two sets of variables. The shaded area in the Venn diagram illustrates the increase in departmental power variance accounted for by value congruity, beyond what is accounted for by the critical contingencies variable. The results are expected to show that the addition of value congruity adds significantly to the explanation of departmental power. The larger the shaded area in figure 4-4, the more significant the unique variance in power accounted for exclusively by value congruity.

Due to the multiple measures of perceived value congruity, critical contingencies and departmental power, separate regression models were necessary to allow for the various operationalizations of the variables. Several models were constructed to examine the incremental explanatory power of value congruity. For convenience and clarity the numerous aspects of the results are tabled in appendix E. Only a summary table reporting the results of partial F tests will be presented in this chapter. Those wishing to examine in greater detail the empirical findings should refer to appendix E.

A Departmental Perspective on Values

The amount of variation in departmental power due exclusively to value congruity was explored from the perspective of departmental units. Different departments evaluated their congruity with top management and the president separately. Results of several regression models revealed that value congruity does provide a unique explanation of variation in power under some, but not all operationalizations of values and power.

Value congruity accounts for additional variation in departmental power

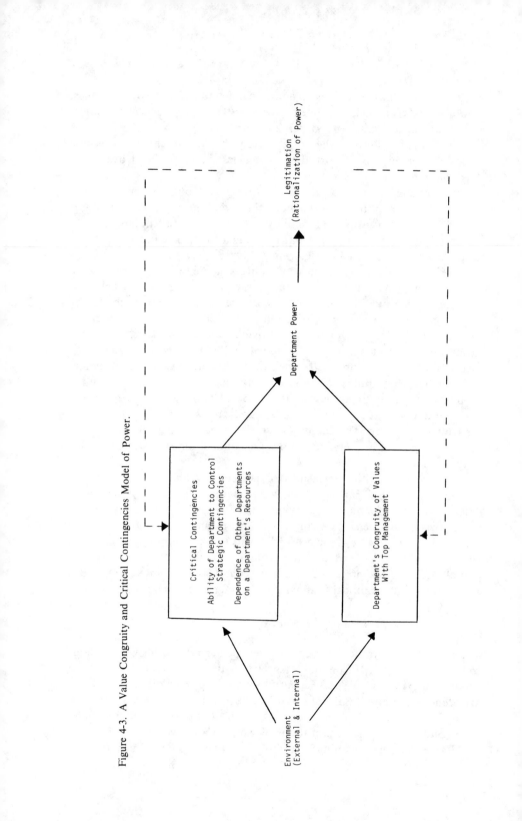

Figure 4-3. A Value Congruity and Critical Contingencies Model of Power.

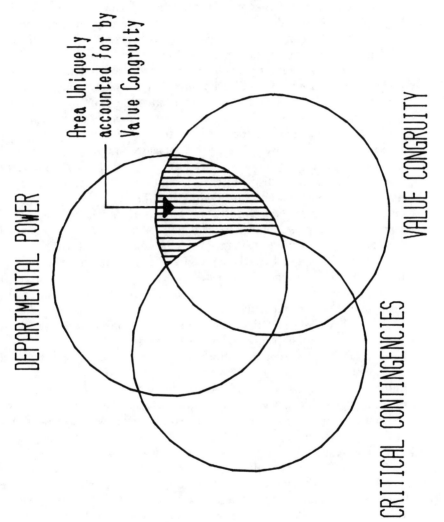

Figure 4-4. Illustration of Variance in Power Uniquely Accounted for by Value Congruity.

when the measure of power is general and congruity is with top management excluding the president. The significance of value congruity was present regardless of the organizational unit assessing departmental power. An example taken from the data will illustrate the explanatory impact of values. When assessing its own general power, 25% of the variation in a department's power was accounted for by control of critical contingencies (see appendix E). This explanation excludes the effects of value congruity on departmental power. When value congruity with top management is added to the regression model, almost 60% of the variance in departmental power is explained. Thus, the variance due to value congruity, over and above that explained by critical contingencies, is around 35%. Clearly, value congruity accounts for more of the variation in departmental power in this situation than does control of critical contingencies. This finding suggests that value congruity does provide a useful supplemental explanation of departmental power.

Not all of the findings indicated that increases in power variance were accounted for by value congruity. When measuring value congruity with the president, and power on distinct issues, insignificant findings were evident. One exception to the insignificant findings was present when a department assessed its own power. For departments evaluating their own power, value congruity with the president does explain power. The president may assume a mythical or symbolic presence that elevates the importance of sharing values in common with him or her. The connection between power and congruity with the president is not demonstrated when top management or other departments assess a department's power. Other groups do not make associations between departmental power and value congruity with the president. They do believe that control of critical contingencies provides a significant explanation of other departments' power.

For top management and other departments, congruity between a department and the president does not uniquely explain power. For these groups a department's power is based on similarity with top management excluding the president. From the perspective of top management, the president may occupy figurehead status and agreement with his values may not be important in determining departmental influence. Top management has greater contact with the president and may attach less mythical significance to his or her values, or may be more aware of this executive's inconsistencies. One manager interviewed discussed his frustrations with the chief executive's inability to translate his values into action by noting, "vision without discipline is a daydream." Top managers may realize that sharing values with the president does not yield the power that congruity with the rest of the top management team does.

The lack of significant findings for congruity with the president may be attributed to the organizational power structure. Top managers, excluding the president, may play the primary roles in conferring power on departments or legitimating the power structure. One final explanation of the insignificant findings is a possible tendency to underrate the importance of values in guiding departmental actions. The policy literature is filled with illustrations of decision-makers who resist acknowledging the role of preferences in influencing organizational actions and who seek economic or rational explanations (Andrews 1980).

Thus, the results of several models provide only partial support for the incremental explanatory contribution of value congruity when congruity of values is examined from the perspective of departmental members. The significance of value congruity in explanations of power becomes more evident when value similarity is evaluated by top management.

Top Management's Perspective on Value Congruity

When top managers perceive a department to share similar organizational values, they also attribute power to that subunit. Value congruity provides increases in departmental power beyond what has been accounted for by critical contingencies. Hence, value similarity serves to explain differences in power beyond explanations using a contingencies approach.

Congruity as perceived by top management is significant in determining departmental power regardless of the party perceiving critical contingencies or the measure of power utilized. Table 4-4 shows five of the six regression models to be significant (i.e. significant partial Fs). The strength of this finding is evident from the consistent results obtained using two measures of power from three different evaluating groups.

The implication of this finding is that power is not just the result of a department's ability to control critical problems, but is also based on shared values as perceived by the executives. Clearly the strong support for this finding provides persuasive evidence for the robustness of the theoretical relationship presented in figure 4-3, particularly given the multiple operationalizations of the dependent and independent variables.

Comparing the findings when top management rather than department members evaluate similarity indicates a stronger connection between congruity and power. Top managers perceive value congruity to provide a greater unique explanation of power than do departmental employees. It is likely that top managers attach greater importance to the sharing of values when they assess power than do departmental employees. Departmental employees may believe power is more directly the result of controlling unknowns, while executives feel that value sharing explains power. Both approaches appear to work together to explain power according to the findings for Roboto and Food King.

Table 4-4.   Partial F Tests on the Unique Explanatory Power
of Value Congruity.

| | Perceptual Measures of Power | | | | | |
| | Own Department | | Top Management | | Other Departments | |
	Issues	General	Issues	General	Issues	General
Departmental Perspective **Perceived Value Congruity**						
With Top Management	2.122 (.158)	27.602 (.0001)	.016 (.899)	3.00 (.096)	.163 (.690)	3.034 (.093)
With the President	6.809 (.015)	2.473 (.128)	.047 (.831)	.092 (.765)	.321 (.576)	.410 (.530)
Top Management Perspective **Perceived Value Congruity**						
With Departments	4.451 (.044)	2.852 (.103)	6.685 (.016)	13.232 (.001)	3.707 (.065)	7.532 (.011)
Latent Value Congruity						
On All Values						
Ranked #1	19.305 (.0002)	.656 (.471)	3.607 (.069)	.180 (.675)	1.470 (.236)	.027 (.870)
Ranked #2	.293 (.593)	1.938 (.176)	.035 (.853)	.127 (.724)	.202 (.657)	1.290 (.266)
On Only the **Important Values**						
Ranked #1	.508 (.483)	.001 (.970)	.054 (.818)	.578 (.454)	1.401 (.247)	.206 (.654)
Ranked #2	.036 (.851)	.046 (.833)	.909 (.350)	.075 (.786)	.086 (.771)	.001 (.973)

Note: The significance levels are presented in parentheses in terms of p values.

Power and Unrecognized Value Congruity

By taking the most important organizational values identified by
departmental members, and comparing these sets of values with the values of
top management, an unrecognized measure of similarity was obtained. Of
particular interest was determining whether unconscious similarity would
determine perceptions of departmental power. Do the unknown, but shared

values between top management and departments determine power beyond what is determined by critical contingencies? The bulk of the evidence from the study of Roboto and Food King suggests that latent values do not provide an incremental explanation of power. If departmental employees or top managers do not consciously express similarity, then the presence of value similarity does not effect evaluations of power.

One exception to the conclusion noted above was present. Latent value congruity on values ranked #1 did provide an additional explanation of the variance in issue-oriented power. The data indicates a negative relationship (Beta weight), suggesting that the greater the unrecognized similarity between a department and top management, the less power the department is perceived to have. Thus, latent congruity is negatively related to power, controlling for the strong positive effects of critical contingencies.

Ignoring for the moment the findings using the perceived measure of congruity, the negative relationships between latent congruity and issue-oriented power may be explained by the importance of risk taking. It is possible that departments are more powerful if they challenge the established values or take chances. If for example a department values support of failures while the rest of the company values stability it may be able to affect specific outcomes to a greater degree than other departments. This ability to effectively control specific issues may explain why the negative relationship was not found between congruity and general power. It is also possible that a department and top management see powerful departments as sharing similar values (strong perceived congruity) when they do not (weak or negative latent congruity). Latent value incongruity combined with expressed similarity may be precursors to power. To be powerful may require that a department has different values from top management, but be perceived as similar.

Other departments' evaluations of power are not significantly explained by latent value congruity. For third parties, control of critical contingencies appears to be a much stronger explanation of power. The role of value similarity in predicting power may also be so intangible as to escape detection by a third party (other department). In addition, it is questionable whether departments asked to evaluate other subunits can do so without being biased by interdepartmental conflict or competition.

Examination of the numerous measures of latent value congruity, summarized in table 4-4, suggests that generally latent value congruity does not account for much of the variance in departmental power when a measure of critical contingencies is present in the equation. Latent value similarity does not explain departmental power as clearly and strongly as perceived control of critical contingencies.

In sum, the only significant findings for the incremental explanatory power of latent value congruity were in a direction opposite that anticipated. Latent value congruity, in some instances, provides a unique explanation of the variance in departmental power as perceived by the department and top management. For other departments, control of critical contingencies provides unique explanatory power while values are insignificant. Values ranked #2 were insignificant determinants of power in all models.

Summary of Findings

Evidence from the study of Roboto and Food King supports the critical contingencies explanation of departmental power. Value congruity has proven to be a useful supplement to this explanation of power. The variation in departmental power uniquely accounted for by value congruity illustrates its promise as an explanatory variable. Thus, both critical contingencies and value congruity are useful determinants of departmental power.

The findings for both perceived and latent measures of value congruity when taken together point to three important results. First, value congruity as perceived by top management provides a better predictor of power than value congruity as perceived by departments. Second, latent value congruity, while generally insignificant, does provide some unique explanation of variance in issue-oriented power. Third, the negative relationship between latent value congruity and power and the positive relationship between perceived value congruity and power once again suggests that the measures of congruity are examining different facets of similarity. In the next section the relationship between perceived and latent congruity will be examined.

The Value Gap and Power

It has been argued throughout this book that value congruity is an important supplement to the critical contingencies explanation of departmental power. Developing indicators of espoused (perceived) value congruity and unrecognized (latent) similarity facilitates the exploration of a third research question. Are perceptions of similarity more strongly associated with power than the unconscious similarity of values?

In this study of Roboto and Food King, it was argued that perceived and latent value congruity may be tapping distinctively different facets of shared values. The unconscious nature of latent value congruity makes this approach a matching of comparison group values. The groups do not know what values the other groups have listed. The members of a subunit are asked to rank their own department's values and top management ranks their own values. These sets of organizational values are matched quantitatively (see chapter 3). Perceived congruity relies on constructed meanings, requiring attributions be made of other groups, and an awareness of the comparison. This approach does not compare value preferences of the two parties, but the espoused similarity. Perceived similarity could be contrived to serve the best interests of top management or the departments involved; hence, espoused congruity may function to conceal rather than reveal similarity.

It is expected that espoused similarity will be more strongly associated with power than will congruity that relies on matching value preferences. This anticipated finding is based in part on a cognitive dissonance logic. For example, if a department is regarded as similar in values to top management, to reduce the possibility of cognitive inconsistency, that department must be evaluated as powerful. Organizational participants are likely to make attributions of power in cases where the department is evaluated as value similar. Note that this argument assumes that power is not driven by the bureaucratic or functional activities of the subunit.

To answer the question of which approach to value congruity, perceived or latent, is more strongly associated with department power, the simple correlations between all of the power and value congruity variables are examined. Examination of the relationships between the various measures of value congruity and power indicates that the perceived measures are more strongly associated with the measures of power than are the latent measures. Of the eighteen correlations between measures of perceived value congruity and measures of power, 83.3% were significant (see table 4-2). Of the twenty-four correlations between latent value congruity and measures of power, 25% were significant.

The only insignificant correlations between perceived congruity and power involved power from the perspective of other departments. The strength of the other fifteen associations ranged from moderate to strong, and all were positive. In contrast, latent congruity on all value statements ranked #2 and the most important value statements ranked #2 were not significantly related to any of the six measures of department power. The strongest correlations between latent similarity and the measures of power involved congruity on only the most important values ranked #1. In sum, the data indicates that perceived value congruity is far more strongly related to power than is latent value congruity.

Why is perceived value congruity more strongly related to power than is latent value congruity? To answer this question requires reflecting on the influence of top management values on the behaviors of organizational participants. Top management (especially the founder) develops a set of values that guide and inform actions in the organization. Because top management is very likely to be a powerful group, department members may express adoption of executive values to increase or perpetuate the departmental standing. Top management desires to impose their values on those in the organization to assure that the firm is operated in a fashion that is consistent with their beliefs and aspirations. Thus, top management sanctions the informal power of departments who espouse their values.

From the perspective of the subunit, expressed value similarity may be a manipulative strategy to increase power. Departments may believe that top management will be more positively disposed toward them (in an attraction sense) if they express similarity. Other motives that guide expressed value similarity may include conflict or anxiety reduction. Departments may express value similarity so as to avoid rocking the boat. By reducing conflict, they negotiate for greater power.

Another explanation of the strong connection between perceived value congruity and power rests with the view that believing is seeing. When departmental members collectively perceive themselves to be similar to top management, for that subunit similarity does exist. This view borrows from the literature on phenomenological sociology (Blumer 1969, Burger & Luckman 1966, Cicourel 1964). The social reality, in this case perceived value congruity, is constructed (not a "real thing out there"). The phenomenological explanation offered here, unlike the ethnomethodological perspective, examines the social context of departments in which members interact to create and perpetuate the perceptions of similarity. Perceived similarity is not an individually created phenomena, but an intersubjective, intradepartmental one. Departmental employees may not know what top management's values are; they reason that they are similar to top management in the absence of knowing.

It is the symbolic communication of agreement with top management values, and not latent congruity, that appears to determine departmental power from the perspective of the departments. For a department, only negative associations are found between unconscious values and power. Rather than adopting and internalizing the same values as top management, powerful departments are those who espouse the same values. This situation does not appear to hold for top management. Executives who espouse similarity of values with a department also unconsciously identify the same values. In essence, top management is more consistent in connecting espoused with unrecognized value similarity. Given this finding, a discussion of how perceived and latent value similarity relate to each other is merited.

Value Consistency and the Value Gap

The results of the studies of Roboto and Food King provide preliminary evidence to indicate the possibility of dramatic differences in the values/power linkage depending on the approach to value congruity. In addition, examining the relationship between perceived and latent value congruity suggests that the intensity of fit between the two approaches is another key to understanding power. Figure 4-5 illustrates two models of the relationships between the forms of congruity and power. The plus and minus signs in the figure indicate positive and negative association.

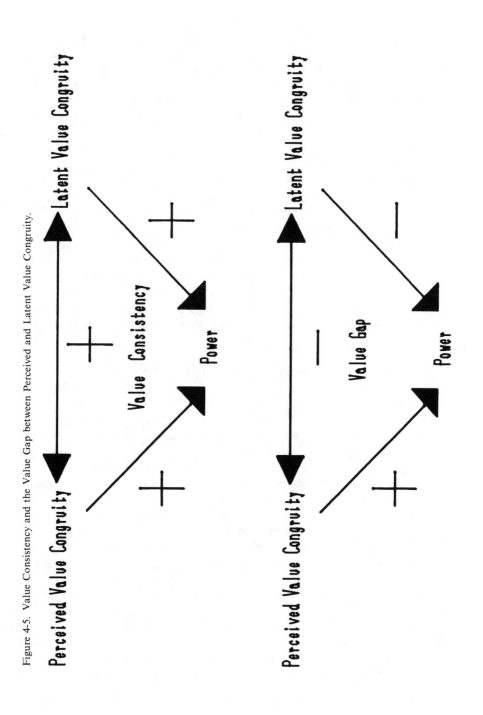

Figure 4-5. Value Consistency and the Value Gap between Perceived and Latent Value Congruity.

If consistency (defined by a positive correlation) exists between perceived and latent value congruity, then both orientations will explain power. The greater the convergence between perceived similarity and unconscious similarity, the more probable that both perceived and latent value congruity will be associated with and explain departmental power. Value consistency suggests that perceptions of similarity fit actual matchings of value preferences for the two groups. In this instance, both facets of congruity are related to a department's power.

When a negative relationship is present between perceived and latent congruity, a value gap exists. The term value gap is used to describe the disparity between perceptions of similarity and unconsciously determined (latent) similarity. A value gap between the facets of congruity will result in only the perceived measure of similarity being significantly related to power. When a department perceives itself to be similar to top management on a set of values, it will also be perceived as powerful. Further, when latent value similarity is not positively associated with perceived value similarity, power will be unrelated or negatively related to latent value congruity. This finding suggests that actually sharing the same values is far less important to being powerful than perceiving that values are shared. It is likely that sharing the same values with top management may be detrimental to departmental power.

The Value Gap and Departmental Perceptions

Of particular interest in the present study is the tendency for the value gap to appear when the department evaluates its own congruity and power but not to exist when other departments and top management assess power. It appears that departments who perceive themselves to be congruent with top management are powerful, while departments who unconsciously share the same values with top management may or may not be powerful depending on the degree of fit or gap between the different orientations to similarity. Departments may not readily internalize the values of the organization, making a gap in expressed and unconscious organizational values possible.

One implication of the value gap is that organizations are not fully in control of any department's values and may not be able to control values or shared meanings at all. Departments work within the corporate culture and manage their expressed values to gain power or rewards, but their true values endure. It may be possible to argue that if departments are to be influential, they must separate themselves from their latent values and join the cultural bandwagon by saying they are similar to top management, even when they are not. It is also possible that departments do not force themselves to abandon their subculture's organizational values, but are simply unaware of the gap between their perceptions of similarity and the values they hold. Finally, departments may experience the unconscious incongruity between their own values and those of top management and express similarity in an attempt to reduce dissonance.

Value Consistency and Top Management

The tentative evidence from the study of Roboto and Food King suggests that top management's perceptions of value similarity fit with an independent calculation of congruity. Departments perceived to be value similar are indeed departments that rank the same values as important. While departmental expressions of similarity with top management do not fit the unconscious similarity, top management expressions do fit latent congruity.

Why do the executives of the companies studied exhibit value consistency? Perhaps a partial explanation is based on the role and position of organizational leaders. Top managers establish the desired organizational values and indeed attempt to socialize employees to adopt these values. The leaders identify with the organization's values, internalize them and are possibly clearer on what values should matter. The greater clarity makes it easier to accurately evaluate similarity. In contrast, departments may be driven by professional values or other values rooted in the society, making it harder to totally accept the guiding values of the firm.

Finally, the evidence presented in the study provides some support for the argument that top managers ultimately evaluate the value congruent departments as powerful. For top managers, those perceived as value congruent and those who unconsciously share the same values are regarded as powerful.

Concluding Note

The findings that have been discussed in this chapter provide both quantitative support for the initial research questions and rich detail based on the qualitative analysis. The study of Roboto and Food King revealed that value congruity is associated with power. Further, value congruity serves as a useful supplement to the popular critical contingencies explanations of power. Finally, the presence of a value gap or fit between different forms of value congruity further clarifies the linkage between values and power.

In the next chapter a case analysis of a medium-sized T-shirt company will be used to illustrate the influence of leader values on organizational decisions.

5

An Illustration: The Case of Weirdware, Inc.

Several years ago, I had the opportunity to work with the employees of a company that was faced with numerous interdepartmental problems. In the process of helping them to improve across departmental relationships, I observed that departmental influence was solidly rooted in value sharing. Sharing the same values as the founders was central to having a voice in organizational issues.

In this chapter, I present the history of Weirdware, Inc. to help illustrate the connection between values and power. Although the company is real, the names of key employees have been changed and some of the facts altered to protect the identity of the firm.

In the Beginning

It all began in 1963 when two guys, Jim ("Weird man") Andrews and his surfing partner, Bud Stafford, got the idea of a business while roaming around a motorcycle show in southern California. Jim, a part-time artist and full-time auto mechanic, was admiring a custom Harley when the idea hit him. "I bet we could make some easy money if we sold T-shirts with wild drawings of bikes on them." Bud, who was attending California State University at Long Beach, agreed mostly because he hated college and wanted an excuse to hang out at the car and bike shows.

This meeting of the minds was the beginning of Weirdware, Inc. Bud took responsibility for the management of the company while Jim provided the "creative genius." Jim still worked as an auto mechanic full-time and Bud dropped out of school to take care of the business.

"No one twisted my arm," recalls Bud; "I was ready to give up on school and this thing looked like it would be fun for a couple of months till I found a real job."

The new entrepreneurs devoted their Friday nights, Saturdays, and Sundays to running a small booth at custom car shows, motorcycle shows, carnivals and fairs. They airbrushed T-shirts with any design the buyer wanted, no matter how obscene or complex. Their specialties included the monster car and funny car designs.

The early sixties were the heyday of "Big Daddy" Roth and Wolfman Jack. Bud and Jim jumped into the southern California culture with gusto. They began to airbrush shirts before the shows and increased the variety of designs and inventory on hand.

In the first year the business was operated from Jim's apartment and Bud's car. When a steady stream of business began coming in, Jim quit his job as a mechanic. Bud had never bothered to find a job after leaving school. Both decided to get serious about the company, which led to the lease of a warehouse, a large loan and the hiring of two of their friends.

"We didn't think this thing would take off like it did; I guess we were just in the right place at the right time," Jim recently commented, adding, "It was fun, we hired our buddies and it was like you could screw around, do what you wanted to do and make a living at the same time." Jim continued, "I hate to say it but we felt like a club or maybe a motorcycle gang; everyone in the company hung out at shows [auto and motorcycle shows]. We smoked, drank, partied and sold T-shirts." Speaking to no one in particular he laughed and said, "Wild, we were wild!"

By the end of the 1960s, Weirdware, Inc. had moved from travelling shows to a mail order business. The owners hired more friends, including their girlfriends. They also changed the operation from airbrushing to silk-screening. The product changed too. With the end of the sixties came the statement T-shirts. Jim and Bud jumped on the bandwagon and began putting political, mostly anti-establishment statements on their shirts. Advertising in *Playboy, Mad Magazine,* and *National Lampoon* yielded amazing increases in sales.

"Most of our business at the time was for drug related stuff—you know the marijuana leaves and cocaine shirts. The political stuff was fun and we liked doing it, but drugs really sold," noted Bud. "This was my generation," added Bud; "I really felt a part of what was happening in the late 60s—my thoughts were all over the U.S. on every kid's back or front."

T-Shirts in the 1970s

Both partners were making more money than they ever expected and began to see the company as a possible long-term, enduring business. "Suddenly in 1970, we decided to get serious," laughed Bud. Jim and Bud were still very casual about business, but getting more interested in the artistic aspects of T-shirt design.

"The artwork was and still is the most important thing to us; the business isn't shit without the designs," remarked Jim.

The early seventies were good times for the company as customer letters illustrate.

Growth was quick and easy during the early 1970s. Although most of the employees were friends of the owners, the company began to take a more "professional" approach. Bud developed an organization chart and placed the marketing, production and finance departments under his supervision. Jim took responsibility for the large art department.

Jim and Bud controlled almost all of the company's affairs, but Wayne Decker supervised the silk-screening process. Wayne was one of the first employees to join the company and knew the way Bud liked things run, perhaps better than Bud knew himself.

"I was a bum, roaming around doing odd jobs when I first met Bud and Jim," recalled Wayne. "I met Bud at a gas station where I was pumping gas. I commented on his T-shirt, I liked it, but told him my grandmother could silk-screen better than the asshole who did that shirt. By the way, Bud had made the shirt," he added. Impulsively Bud hired Wayne to silk-screen T-shirts.

In the 1970s, Bud and Jeff took an aggressive approach to the market and expanded into license agreements with two motorcycle manufacturers. In addition, they expanded into imprinted underwear. Their advertising, still brash and wild, became more polished and their target audience expanded.

In 1974, the company had forty-five employees and revenues around $800,000. Bud and Jim were beginning to realize that they needed some full-time assistance in the financial aspects of the company, so they hired an accountant, Jeff Hallander.

"Jeff was a nice 'straight' type of guy. It may sound cruel but Jeff was like a recruiting poster for The Nerds," noted Bud. "At the time we thought he was kinda strange, but we really needed him."

Recently Jeff noted, "My entire family thought I was nuts going to work for this garage business where all the employees were high on drugs and hated the establishment."

Jeff was not alone in his perceptions of the company. A longtime supplier of T-shirts noted, "They were anything but conventional in the 1960s and 70s. There were always rumors that the two owners were dealing drugs, which they never did, but the place was full of dropouts and dopers."

The Company Today

By 1980 Bud and Jim were millionaires and the organization had grown to a company of over 500 employees. The organization had gone through several reorganizations and introduced a more professional approach to marketing and customer service. Weirdware had moved away from the written word on a

Figure 5-1. Weirdware, Inc.: Organization Chart, 1970.

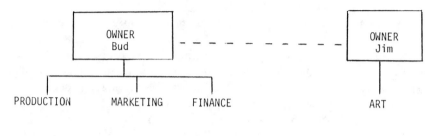

Table 5-1.   Letters from Customers.

Dear Whoever,

You're shirts are great! I love the one that says "Good Ass is Hard to Find" mainly because I have a large ass! Keep those shirts coming.

Sue
Tempe, Az.

Dear Sirs:

I am a young man who must hang out! If I wear anything at all, I might as well hang out in your designs. I really liked your advertisement on page 45 of the September issue of the National Lampoon. When I get my bucks together I will send for one of those shirts.

Pat
Muncie, Ind.

Gentlemen:

It would be deemed a most sincere honor to be accorded the receipt of a copy of your extravagant and glorious catalog delineating the weird, bizarre, sublime and benign creations of the highest heads in all of California. Sitting here in rapt expectoration, I remain your most truly humble servant.

GSA
New York, N.Y.

T-shirt and followed the trend into graphic designs. While silk screening was still the basic technology for the business, expansion had made it possible for them to provide T-shirts to department stores.

"What scared me in 1983 was realizing that our business was now legitimate," commented Jim. "We even hired our first M.B.A.! I remember when everyone stayed up late drinking beer and doing drugs to get the orders finished. Some say we sold drugs, but we have never done that; we do believe in recreational chemicals and we did put water pipes in with large orders ten years ago."

Bud quickly clarified, "We don't put pipes in with our shipments anymore, we can't afford it! Seriously, we stopped doing that," added Bud. "Things have changed a lot since the 1960s, but we are still very unique."

"What Bud means is we are still weird," Jim noted with a smile of pride.

Almost all of the T-shirt silk screeners have ten to twenty years with the company. "We were all hippies back then, and now, well I guess many of us are just old hippies," says Jim. He continues to hold on to this part of the company's culture by keeping a plastic marijuana plant in his office and he still wears jeans every day. A large percentage of the employees wear T-shirts to work every day, and the art department is full of "Very Weird People."

Bud has redesigned the organization, primarily because of the growth of the firm. Figure 5-2 shows the organization chart in 1984. This design has preserved the direct reporting relationship between Jim and the art department. As Jim noted, "Art is special in this business and I'm not willing to let this part of the business slip away from me."

The playful atmosphere still pervades the company, but not all departments seem to share the same enthusiasm. The customer service people don't seem to have time to fool around because they are taking orders constantly. The accountants wear shirts and ties and refuse to look like teenagers. As one accountant noted, "It's just not professional going to work dressed like a slob."

Another new employee commented, "I occasionally apologize at parties because of the stupid name of this place. People remember the business from the days when the packers put water pipes in with every T-shirt order."

Even the most casual of observers will notice a great deal of variation in style of dress, approach to work and general outlook. Jim, with a serious frown on his face begins, "Some of our departments are filled with people who, who are OK, I mean they do their job, but they just don't understand the soul of the T-shirt business."

"Yeah," Bud adds, "they think they know what's good for the business, strategic planning, coping with a changing market and all that, but we know what we want this company to be."

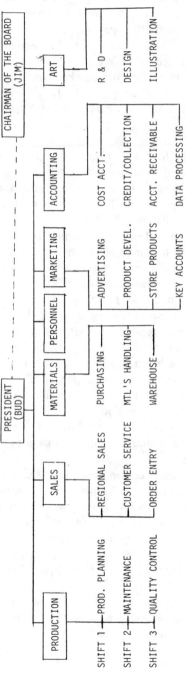

Figure 5-2. Weirdware, Inc.: Organization Chart, 1984.

"In fact, some groups of people around here, and I won't name any particular department, actually advise us to put our money in something besides T-shirt products," commented Jim with wonder. "They think they have our best interests at heart, but we don't want to be in any other business. We don't know any other business."

"Yeah, and we're too dumb to try," added Jim.

The Question of Influence

Knowing a little about the culture at Weirdware, Inc., we can now raise the question of departmental influence. Knowing what is important to the top managers, which departments are most likely to wield influence in the decision making process?

According to the critical contingencies perspectives, the department most able to provide critical resources or cope with the critical environmental unknowns will have power. One of the current unknowns at Weirdware, Inc., revolves around technological advances that facilitate different imprinting techniques. Repeatedly the art department personnel, sometimes en masse with all the art people standing in the executive offices, have told Jim and Bud that the business is based on silk-screening and for artistic integrity must remain true to the technique.

As the director of art recently remarked, "This business is based on design. Look at any T-shirt produced using the new technology and you will see a poor quality product. You simply cannot have a good T-shirt, in terms of graphic clarity and quality, if you depart from the silk-screen process."

Production disagrees. As one shop supervisor noted, "We are slow, labor intensive, and have terrible waste problems. The equipment we use is from the stone age! I cannot understand why we waste so much damn money on an inferior process." But their arguments fall on deaf ears and the company ignores new innovations in design imprinting.

Finance also appears to be helpless in influencing how things are done at Weirdware. This department's personnel are concerned with the current fixed costs; particularly the existence of a R & D group within art is a cost drain with little or no return. One clerk noted, "I see the bills that come in, I know how much we make and I don't know why they don't cut some of the extra stuff."

The controller expressed a similar concern: "If the company is to remain financially viable the expenses must be cut."

Jim and Bud have been informed by the art department that finance doesn't understand what is important in this type of business. Jim and Bud agree with the art group and the philosophy that you have to put more money into the creative aspects of the business. Jim defensively argues, "It's our money and we want it in art!"

Marketing is perhaps the most critical department because of the changing needs of the customer. Once again the opinions of the art department prevail. Frustrated salesmen constantly complain that the company will not survive if they do not respond to the cultural changes in American society. As one regional sales representative observes, "Our designs were perfect ten years ago, but they don't sell in today's market."

What department has the most influence in Weirdware? Clearly the powerful group is the art department and they influence decisions in every realm, not just art. As one accountant put it, "If you aren't in the art department here your opinion isn't worth shit."

A marketing person confirmed the view, noting, "Jim and Bud, they listen, but you can tell that they favor art. People in that department can do no wrong, everything is art art art. It's really short sighted of them I think. After all, the business isn't art anymore, it's distribution," argued the marketer.

Final Note

The opinions of experts monitoring this industry reveal that the art area is not where critical unknowns can be controlled or important resources managed. Rationally and strategically, the concerns and areas of greatest impact are in technological change and marketing.

The models of power reviewed in previous chapters point to two political models. In keeping with the contingencies model the most powerful department in Weirdware should be marketing, because this subgroup has the ability to control the greatest uncertainties. However, control of critical uncertainties, such as knowledge of customer preferences, does not dictate departmental power in this small company. The connection between control of critical environmental uncertainties and departmental power is nonexistent. Observing Weirdware mitigates the argument for control of critical contingencies as an explanation of power.

Conversations with Jim and Bud suggest that survival is of little importance to them. What they value is the artistic component of the business and this guides their decisions and the informal power network as well.

The model of value sharing I have presented earlier in this book would explain the Weirdware case as an example of organizational values influencing behaviors and subsequently the power of one department. Clearly the art department was in a position to influence the opinions of top management and get their way. Of the two political models, the cultural one is supported by the illustrative information available on Weirdware. The art department, as a unit, operates with the same set of organizational values as top management; hence, it is the most powerful subgroup.

Is Weirdware unique? In many respects it is different from other businesses. Is the role of value sharing also unique to this company? It appears evident from the study of Food King and Roboto, in addition to the case of Weirdware, that what drives these and many other small companies is a set of organizationally specific values or preferences regarding what we ought to be doing and how we ought to do it. Thus, values appear to guide organizational functioning and departmental power in seemingly irrational and occasionally unpredictable ways.

6

Summary and Conclusions

Given the relative newness of the value congruity construct and the cultural paradigm in the study of organizations, it would be premature to attempt a definitive explanation of the ramifications of the study reported in this book. It is only through further empirical testing and measurement development that the results of the study can be validated and extended. The results of interviews and field surveys in Roboto and Food King have only scratched the surface in our understanding of organizational values.

Going beyond the findings, I will offer some conclusions that reinforce the essential centrality of values to the functioning of any organization. It is my opinion that departmental power cannot be understood without considering value congruity. Indeed, we cannot make sense out of organizational actions without values. It is my hope that researchers will begin to systematically study organizational values as antecedents and consequences of other organizational phenomena.

In this final chapter the implications of the study results will be discussed. I will indulge in some speculative conclusions about the role of values in organizational study and offer some questions for further consideration. The chapter will conclude with a brief attempt at synthesizing the value congruity and strategic contingencies approaches to power.

How Important Are Values?

Organizational values are very important to corporate success, according to the recent practitioner literature (Peters & Waterman 1982). Books and articles over the last three years have argued that highly effective companies foster values and create a culture (Deal & Kennedy 1983, Hickman & Silva 1984, Peters & Austin 1985). Consultants have jumped on the bandwagon with attempts to help companies change their cultures (Short & Farratt 1984, Silverzweig & Allen 1976), control their cultures (Kilmann 1982), or strategically plan around their cultures (Tichy 1982). A *Business Week* article that appeared shortly after corporate culture replaced Theory Z as the latest buzz word for managers cited company after company where clearly articulated values resulted in profits and growth. Overwhelmingly the business community has embraced the importance of values and the necessity of examining corporate culture.

What should we make of all the armchair speculation on the critical role of values? Carroll (1983), in a review of *In Search of Excellence,* deflates the values and culture balloon by arguing that it is full of hot air. Specifically, he suggests that the proof Peters and Waterman offer for a corporate values-success connection is grounded in anecdotes, secondary sources of support, and unexplained research.

It is precisely the faddish nature of the popular writing on the topic and the legitimate arguments of Mr. Carroll (among others) that makes the present study a contribution to understanding values. Practitioners and consultants have unearthed an important facet of organizational functioning, but their argument is not supported by systematic inquiry. The study of Roboto and Food King is an attempt to seriously examine the role of values. The research reported here endeavored to go beyond common sense wisdom and anecdotal information to empirical testing. Separating organizational from work and personal values, and devising a measure of value congruity were the necessary first steps.

Examinations of values to date have focused on identification of the "right" set of values. Peters and Waterman (1982) identify seven dominant beliefs an excellent company should have. Miller (1984) devotes an entire book to presenting eight primary values to foster the American corporate spirit. Rather than force employees to adopt a set of values outsiders suggest are "right," executives who wish to shape their company's culture should examine the fit of values between various groups. It is the sharing and not the specific values that explain how organizations function.

How important are values in the functioning of the firm? Clearly, they help to explain departmental power, as the results summarized in chapter 4 have shown. If a department's values are at variance with top management's, departmental actions will not support the values of top management and the department will not be able to influence outcomes, even if it controls critical contingencies.

What other facets of organizational functioning are explained by value sharing? This question deserves further consideration and will require researchers to separate the important issues from the spurious ones. What are the effects of value divergence? Must subgroups with diverse values be integrated? If departments must be value similar, how do organizational leaders accomplish this objective? Under what circumstances is value congruity essential? What ultimate gain is achieved by value congruity?

Some argue that in the corporation of today, efforts to elicit commitment and involvement require selling employees on the values of the company. The task for executives is to behave consistently so that the espoused values are the values in action. If a value gap exists between a department's perceptions of similarity and their latent value similarity, top management must examine the reasons why. This view raises the question, is it desirable for executives to provide a consistent value direction to insure that a department's espoused values fit its latent values? Is it undesirable to have a value gap? Can commitment and satisfaction be heightened by value consistency? Once again, many questions remain to be answered.

A Cultural Approach

A great deal of attention and criticism has been given to the assumptions underlying traditional organizational analysis (Burrell & Morgan 1979). Louis (1981) contrasted the assumptions of the traditional approach to organizational science (e.g. structure at the macro level) with the assumptions of a cultural perspective. She argues that a cultural approach focuses on understanding actions that emerge from shared meanings (Louis 1981, 1983). Researchers define culture as a set of common values that are expressed in symbols (Dandridge, Mitroff & Joyce 1980), rituals (Beyer & Trice 1984) stories (Wilkins 1983) and language (Evered 1983). Unfortunately, many have become fixated on examining the cultural artifacts (e.g. symbols and stories) and completely ignore common values.

The argument for a cultural perspective to organizational analysis is usually framed with a discussion of what traditional organization theory has failed to do. Inherent in the traditional approaches is the assumption that behavior is determined by the technology and the structure of the organization (Pondy & Mitroff 1979). Interest has centered on matching organizational strategies and goals with the appropriate structure, technology and environmental constraints. These are important considerations in understanding organizations, but not sufficient. These models have failed to examine how people collectively make sense of their organizational life.

Pondy and Mitroff (1979) advocate the introduction of a new approach, a cultural model, to the field of organizational theory. These authors criticize the dominant models guiding organizational research for being simple and static. They make the case for directing our attention to different issues and "also away from others" (1979, 11). The critique of organizational theory is expressed by Starbuck (1982, 7) as follows:

> The dramatic successes of physical science over the last 200 years have inspired much admiration by social scientists. These imitations have generally succeeded socially but failed substantively: they have won prestige and achieved prevalence even though they have concentrated upon superficial analyses of ephemeral phenomena.

The criticisms of existing models of organizations is the foundation upon which cultural approaches have been built. Organizations do not operate under simple rules of reasonableness, but often operate as a function of the enduring values shared by organizational participants. A cultural approach is important because it offers a different explanation for what goes on in organizations. The virtue of the concept of culture is its potential to complement the existing body of knowledge regarding organizations and allow for expansion on previously ignored components.

The cultural model of power presented in chapter 1 argued that the sharing of organizational values determines subunit power. In doing so, the study departs from the assumption that organizations exist in a concrete objective reality. Concentration on value congruity as a determinant of power involved measuring and testing a relatively unexplored component of organizations. As the results indicate, value congruity is a meaningful predictor of departmental power. Explanatory usefulness of value congruity exists, even when the more popular explanations of power are taken into consideration.

The importance of this study goes beyond the examination of an unexplored variable. By examining value congruity as a supplementary, not competing explanation for departmental power, the study attempts to blend existing models grounded in the functionalist tradition with a new variable originating from an interpretive framework.

Pfeffer (1981b) argues that organizations should be analyzed on two levels; one affecting substantive outcomes such as allocation of budgets (e.g. critical contingencies), the other affecting symbolic outcomes (e.g. values). In his opinion these two levels have different dependent variables and different processes. This book has attempted to argue the contrary position and provide evidence to suggest that the symbolic facets of organizations do effect substantive areas such as power.

Future theorizing should not ignore the impact of symbolic activities on actual outcomes of organizations. In keeping with those who have espoused a cultural perspective, I believe organizations should be viewed as systems of shared meanings in which realities are socially constructed. The distinction drawn in this study between latent and perceived value congruity is an attempt to examine in greater detail how differing conceptions of value similarity influence power. The greater predictive power of perceived versus latent measures of congruity may indicate the importance of created realities and suggest more theoretical attention be given to the force of group consensus and the social construction process in organizations.

In summary, the findings of the study reported in this book add support to the existing theoretical arguments that suggest values are important but hidden facets of organizational functioning. Theoretical work that acknowledges the importance of studying values is only the first step. What is needed now is further empirical investigation of values and how value congruity impacts on various organizational variables.

Limitations of the Study

The level of analysis for this study is the department, an easily identifiable unit. This unit of analysis may be problematic if it masks intradepartmental groupings. For Roboto and Food King no distinction was drawn between membership in the structurally determined subunit (department) and the culturally defined subunit (see Fine & Kleinman 1979 and Fine 1979 for a treatment of subcultures). The existence of several subgroups within a department may limit the role of values at the departmental level. Although evidence was presented to suggest that the department was a meaningful unit of analysis, future research should investigate the role of values in various informal groups. The use of network analysis and sociometrics would prove useful in determining social groupings. Examination of groupings according to level in the organization may also prove to be a useful focus for future study. It may be more important for managers to be value congruent with top management than for subordinates to share values.

Implicit in the study was the assumption that values are primarily the result of the social setting. This view tends toward an oversocialized conception of man, by ignoring individual differences and stressing the role of socialization (see Wrong 1961 for a more involved explanation of oversocialized man). It was the intention of this study to show that power is the result of more than just adapting to environmental problems. A movement away from structural explanations of power is a step toward bringing "man" back into the analysis of power. At the same time this study does not consider power or values other than those shared in the context of organizations. In addition the study does not explore possible motives for value congruity. Research into how individual bases of power and values interact with departmental power and value congruity is needed. Examination of the many motives for expressed value congruity would also prove valuable.

Finally, the study is cross-sectional, making it impossible to make causal statements concerning the relationship between values and power. All that can be determined in this study are the associations among the various variables for the specific companies. In addition, future research should attempt to refine these measures of values, with an awareness of the difficulty of operationalizing the concepts.

Conclusions

My observations in the two companies studied here and subsequent organizations has led me to some general conclusions. By observing and listening to employees I have become more committed to the dominant role that value sharing plays in organizational behavior and design. I will offer some specific conclusions that come out of this research activity.

First and most important, all social interaction is infused with shared values. This conclusion highlights the social constructionist view that organizational members symbolically create an ordered world (Meyer & Rowan 1977, Morgan 1980). Social facts are the construction of shared interaction not a world out there separate from the actors (Mills 1972). Reality is intersubjective or known through others. This common experience helps to explain why perceived value sharing can shape attitudes and guide actions. Value attributions are made to the organization and its leaders, and perceptions of similarity serve as a guide and legitimator of behavior. The organizational values provide a shared way of seeing the world, and, at the same time, a way of not seeing the world.

Second, organizational values survive long after founders, despite changes in organizational design. Cultures are not just the personalities of the chief executive or the idiosyncrasies of the president. Cultures are enduring and independent of organizational leaders (Barley 1983). The organization may change its structure, its environment, or its technology; but the shared values about how things are done here and what is valued tend to endure. This is not to suggest that organizational values never change; they do, but slowly. Top managers' beliefs are critical, as the study results suggest. However, the further the leaders deviate from the historically stated values, the harder it is for them to dictate actions. Leaders and followers alike are in large part slaves of the past. This conclusion helps to explain why the successful companies have such strong histories and why value change is so difficult. Because organizations are infused with values and these values survive over long periods, it makes sense for leaders to impose order on value sharing by concentrating on the articulation of values. This insight is perhaps the greatest contribution consultants have attempted to present to executives.

As a third conclusion, some organizational values are unique and some are held in common by numerous organizations. There are always some values at the very core of an organization that are unique. Yet, not all of the critical organizational values are unique to a firm. Some values are shared by many different and diverse firms. In the companies studied here, some values were unique in their importance, but others were shared in common. Some values are unique to the organization, while others are unique to the industry, market, region of the country, and so forth. Some values may be a product of

American or Western societies (e.g. rationality and equality). It is also possible that the generality of some values depends on the level of the organization examined. For example, managers in different companies may share general values as a result of M.B.A. programs or professional associations. Lower level employees (and many top executives) may rely on more organization specific values.

The next conclusion I wish to assert is that within any organization it is possible to identify subcultures. Most organizational theorists who are interested in culture have argued that organizations must be viewed as multicultural (Gregory 1983, Louis 1983). As the interviews in Roboto and Food King revealed, departments exist with different values. Given the specific nature of problem-solving in different departments, it is not surprising that unique value sets would exist. Lawrence and Lorsch (1969) argued cogently that successful firms try to maintain departmental differences and also integrate. Value sharing is one mechanism for both differentiation and integration. Regardless of the distinguishing factors, departments share distinctive values that help determine what is important and what behaviors are acceptable.

The final conclusion I wish to offer is that top management's values influence all departments. If a department becomes too divergent in their values, the organizational leaders will attempt to change, or restrict the department. The values of top management typically are the most commonly accepted within the organization. As noted earlier, executives are slaves to the organization's historical values and cannot easily alter the guiding preferences. Subunits that express values in conflict are defined as counter-cultures. If these counter-cultures become threatening for the leaders, action will be taken to alter, constrain or break up this group.

This conclusion suggests that every firm is faced with both the functional and dysfunctional outcomes of value congruity. The functional aspects of value congruity might be increased cooperation and increased commitment. The numerous practitioner articles suggest that value congruity results in increased organizational commitment, effectiveness, and job satisfaction (Schmidt & Posner 1983, Deal & Kennedy 1981). The dysfunctional effects may include groupthink, increased conformity, decreased dissent, a lack of creativity, or an inability to adapt to environmental changes. Shared values may spawn a homogeneous work group which could result in groupthink (see Janis 1972) or deindividuation (see Festinger, Pepitone & Newcomb 1952). Homogeneity may hamper an organization's ability to respond to environmental change. An organization with strong value congruity may ignore information provided by departments with incongruent values and exert pressure on dissenting departments to guard against information not in accord with organizationally shared values. Through self selection and socialization, shared values can be used to rationalize the existing power structure and decision-making strategies. Thus value congruity can perpetuate the status quo and seriously hinder adaptation and change.

The main theme pervading my conclusions is that sense making in organizations cannot occur without considering the important role of values and value sharing. Out of this set of conclusions comes a synthesis of the value congruity and critical contingencies perspectives on power.

A Synthesis of Value Congruity and Critical Contingencies

The conclusion derived in the previous section, that value congruity informs all actions in organizations, suggests a rethinking of determinants of power. Arguing that value sharing is pervasive requires that values have temporal precedence in any model of power. Value congruity assumes a prominent position in developing an explanation of power. Using this logic, critical contingencies are defined in the context of value sharing. Since all departments do not share the same organizational values, agreement on what is critical is impossible. It is the departments who share values with top management that are in a position to define what contingencies are critical. Thus power is not accrued to those subunits who are most capable of coping with unknowns; rather, power is acquired by departments who define the unknowns.

A new model of power displayed in figure 6-1 suggests causality, and indicates value sharing as a precursor to critical contingencies explanations of power. Control of resources and coping with uncertainty cannot be linked to departmental power unless the subunit is capable of defining what is critical. Value congruity facilitates the defining of what is critical. By espousing similar values, a department is in a better position to participate in the defining of contingencies. The model indicates that value congruity can lead directly to power or serve as a context in which to define what is critical. Whether value sharing leads directly or indirectly to departmental power, its central role cannot be overlooked.

Once power is obtained, departments try to legitimate the power by referring back to value congruity. Legitimation is a process by which the actions of a department are defined as acceptable, right, or appropriate (Epstein 1969). Relying on their shared preferences for organizational action, departments attempt to legitimate the acquisition of their power. It is for this reason that legitimation of power feeds back to value congruity in the model in figure 6-1. Hence, the department finds it necessary to justify its exercise of power by calling upon the appropriateness of the values shared with those who lead the firm (see Weber 1947 for a detailed discussion of bases of legitimation). The appropriateness of the power rests in the ability of a

Figure 6-1. Synthesis of Value Congruity and Critical Contingencies.

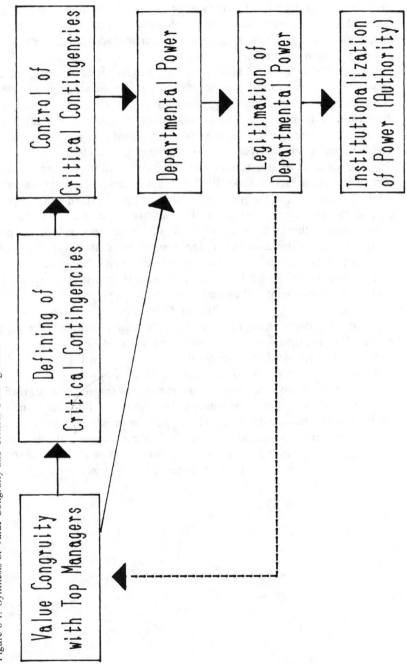

department to attach its actions to the historically legitimate values of the firm. Past congruity will effect present values and definitions of contingencies that will in term impact on future power relationships. The legitimation of power is a means by which unstable power can be made stable. Departmental power is temporary until it is legitimated.

A specific department of a firm may try to convince other departments and top management that its power is legitimate by showing that the subunit can control unknowns. This attempt will fail unless others are receptive to the department's definition of critical unknowns. Receptivity is a function of value preference and thus a vicious cycle of perpetuating existing departmental power is revealed to the incongruent subunit.

The ultimate legitimation of power is its institutionalization, as the last component of the model shows. Pfeffer (1981b) notes that institutionalization is the process whereby the power of a department is defined and accepted as part of the organization's culture. Formal organizational rules that grant departments authority grow out of the legitimation process. Political power or the informal influence of a department must at this point become transformed or domesticated into rational authority (Weiss & Enz 1985). Thus, departmental power has come full circle from a temporary ability to control to a permanent right to influence.

Critical contingencies on the surface appear to provide a logical explanation of departmental power. What the model presented here suggests is that this explanation cannot stand on its own. Power can only be understood in terms of value congruity. Further, it has been reasoned that political power either fades or becomes stable as authority.

In sum, value congruity has been virtually unexplored in organizational research, but can no longer be ignored. The significant findings of the study reported in this book indicate the viability of the construct; however there is much to be learned about the usefulness of values in organizational settings. The virtue of considering value congruity rests with its potential to complement and expand our understanding of organizations.

Appendix A

Methodology

This study represents a combination of exploratory research on values and value congruity, and hypotheses testing regarding the relationship between values and departmental power. Two companies were selected for study: Food King, a national fast service chain of restaurants, and Roboto, a young high technology company. Food King is publicly owned and Roboto is a venture capital organization. The study was conducted during 1984 and 1985, and involved two stages of data collection. The first stage of the study involved interviews and observations. The second stage included the administration of a survey to all employees of the two companies.

Data Collection Stage 1: Interviews

The first stage of analysis involved interviews with critical personnel. In both organizations all department heads, a random sample of departmental personnel, and all top managers (including the presidents) were interviewed. In addition, field personnel in three regional locations of Food King were interviewed.

Data were collected using structured, open-ended interview questions. The interviews consisted of ten formal questions and seventeen structured probes or extending questions. Interview guide forms (see appendix B) were used to record interview data. Coding of the information involved transcribing each question for each interviewee. The transcribed lists were then coded to determine the frequency of various themes or issues.

The purposes of the interviews were (1) to enhance the understanding of the constructs, (2) improve conceptual clarity, and (3) facilitate development of the survey. Interviews enhance understanding by offering flexibility in questioning and allowing for clarifying and expanding the constructs. The interactive quality of these interviews provided insight into how subjects view the topics of values, critical contingencies and power.

The seventeen probes were developed in advance of the interview and served two purposes. First, the probe focused discussion on the topics of interest in the study and second, the probes allowed the respondents to extend or clarify their prior statements.

The validity of statements was checked by observing behavioral cues of the subjects. At the end of each interview the researcher completed an affect checklist (see appendix B). The checklist was used to record any unusual dynamics in the interview that might bias the interviewee's statements or the interviewer's interpretation. Evaluations of the clarity of the questions and the general attitude of the respondent were also included in the affect checklist. Later reference to the checklists for each individual interviewed allowed the interviewer to check for possible behavioral or interaction bias. The criticality of any issue was determined by examining how frequently the issue was mentioned. When numerous respondents identified the same issue or value, the relevance of the statement increased.

All interview data were coded twice by the researcher as a check on the reliability of the issues. Reliability and validity of coding was enhanced by following the suggestions of Crittenden and Hill (1971). To improve coding, the interview information was specific and the location of information was defined by the interview guide's design. The interviews were conducted by a single investigator, reducing differences in data collection due to interviewer variability.

Finally, the interview stage improved conceptual clarity by insuring that the respondents understood and interpreted the questions properly. This portion of the study was exploratory and findings were used to improve the second stage of the study. The interviews served as a pretest device for the questionnaire to improve clarity of questions and relevance to the organization under study. Responses to interview questions were used to develop and customize the survey.

Interview Questions

Interview questions focused on three areas of concern: (1) values, (2) critical contingencies, and (3) power. A list of the ten general questions was provided to each respondent before beginning the interview. Interviewees were also provided a list of departments to assist them in answering questions oriented toward departmental differences.

Values

Values are based on cultural knowledge or meanings acquired in the organizational context. To examine values, the researcher must develop an understanding of how subjects view the construct. In keeping with symbolic interactionists (Blumer 1969), values are viewed in this study as a product of a shared system of meanings; learned, revised, maintained, and defined in the context of the specific organization studied. Use of interviews to gain insight into contextually determined values is critical if this study is to avoid the pitfalls of the existing value literature that relies on values that may not be a part of the subjects' value set. (For a critique of existing measures see Zenzen & Hammer 1980)

Values were examined in two ways. First, a general question asked interviewees to list the most and least important values a company should have in running a business. Respondents were asked whether the lists were similar to their own beliefs and if there were departments whose beliefs were similar or dissimilar to theirs. A final probe asked whether their values were similar to those of top management.

The term top management elicited different responses depending on whether the subjects defined top management to mean the president or to represent department heads and vice presidents. The question was broken down into two parts representing these two categories of top management in order to clarify interviewee interpretation and improve the questions. This alteration was made early in the interview process.

The second measure of values was obtained using a card sort. Twenty-seven value statements were typed on index cards. Each subject was asked to sort the cards into two piles. In one pile the interviewees were to place the five most important values a company should have in running a business. In another pile the respondents were to place the five least important values. Additional important values, absent from the card sort, were solicited from employees, as well as comments concerning how they picked the values they selected in each category. Subjects were asked whether the list would be different if they sorted the values according to what their company values versus what a company should value. Early in the interview process additional values were added to the card sort based on the comments of subjects.

Critical Contingencies

Critical contingencies are those problem areas that are considered most important for an organization's success. The list of critical problems will vary depending on the task environment of a company. Defining critical contingencies requires learning about the problems of a company's industry as well as problems unique to the organization.

Strategic contingencies were determined by questions focusing on major problems Food King and Roboto encountered in their industries and the criticality of these problems to their success. Probes examined how the companies dealt with the critical problems and which departments were most involved or necessary in solving the problems.

Another approach to strategic contingencies involved asking respondents what things were the most unpredictable or uncertain in their industry. Probing questions were used to distinguish whether unknowns occur regularly or have a consistent pattern. Following the work of Hinings et al. (1974), problem areas found to have unpatterned variation were considered the most relevant uncertainties for the organizations in the survey stage. After numerous interviews it was evident that interviewees did not draw a distinction between critical problems and industry unknowns. Issues identified as critical were also considered unpredictable.

Resource dependence was investigated by noting that departments don't just take from the firm, but also provide resources for the company. Resources were defined as things like information, people, skills, and sales. Respondents were asked, "What are some of the resources that departments provide the company?" Probes focused on the importance, criticality and scarcity of the resources. Respondents consistently had difficulty listing resources. When resources were stated, the lists were descriptions of departments' functional activities. Interviewees, including top managers, were unable to list resources controlled by departments that fell outside of their areas of responsibility. Numerous probes were unsuccessful in revealing a list.

Past research on resource dependence (Pfeffer & Salancik 1974) begins by providing a list of critical resources and then asks interviewees to specify the importance of the a priori list. That research does not provide an explanation of how the investigators arrived at their list of critical resources. It may be easier to generate a list of resources if the organization studied is one you are familiar with and a member of, as was the case for Pfeffer and Salancik. In the case of this study, generation of an a priori list of critical resources would be too arbitrary to be of value. Because of the confusion in answering the resource dependence question, it was dropped from the interview guide and the collection of information on critical contingencies was provided by the strategic contingencies questions.

Power

Department power was operationalized in this study as the ability to affect the outcomes of other departments. To obtain information on power, questions were asked about which departments have the ability to affect the outcomes of other departments, why, and when. Information concerning the situationality of influence and the departments least able to affect others was obtained through probing questions. Use of the term ability to affect outcomes was frequently restated as influence by respondents when answering questions. Providing a general assessment of department influence was an easy task by interviewees in both companies.

Data Collection Stage 2: Surveys

In the second stage of the study a survey was administered to all corporate personnel in both companies. The management team in Food King's regional stores was also surveyed as were two subordinates from each store. Questionnaires were distributed by intraoffice mail to all corporate personnel and by the regional offices in the case of store personnel of Food King. Respondents returned their completed surveys directly to the researcher via the mail. A special set of questions was mailed directly to each top manager soliciting information on top management perceptions of value congruity.

The purpose of this portion of the study is to examine determinants of perceived departmental power. In addition, the survey is an attempt to begin inquiry into the role of values and value congruity in organizations. The two objectives of the survey are: (1) explanation of departmental power and (2) exploration of a new explanatory variable—value congruity.

Sample

Questionnaires were received from 447 persons in Food King, of which 356 were usable, and from fifty-eight persons in Roboto. In both companies the corporate personnel completed the survey and returned it directly via the mail. Field personnel returned the surveys directly to me or to their regional manager, who sent them, stapled, to me.

The response rate for Food King corporate personnel was 55% (N=57) and 58% (N=58) for Roboto. Field personnel response for Food King was 57% (N=389). The response rate, while not extremely large, was good given the length and complexity of the survey. In both companies performance pressures and time constraints placed on employees make it difficult to justify taking the survey. Endorsement letters from the presidents of the companies and a follow-up letter may have contributed to the moderately good response rates. Top management's response rate was 100% in both companies.

The average member of the Food King sample was a single, 27 year old male who has attended but not graduated from college. For Roboto, the average respondent was a 31 year old male, and a college graduate. Top managers from Food King were on the average 31 years old and college graduates. Roboto's top managers were older (38 was the average age) and more educated, with 50% having masters and Ph.D.'s.

Measures

The survey included measures of values, value congruity, critical contingencies and department power. The measures were developed and revised as a direct result of the interview findings.

Values

The objective of the present study is to measure the congruity of organizationally related values between top management and departments. A review of existing measures of values (see table A-1) suggests that the personal, interpersonal, moral, or work related measures are not appropriate to meet all three of the measurement criteria of secular, work related and organizationally focused values.

The difficulty with the scales listed in table A-1 is their lack of applicability to an organizationally centered approach to measuring values. Work related values (Wollack et al. 1971) are concerned with beliefs about a person's job, not preferences for organizational actions or outcomes. Some value measures focus on universal values such as kindness, honesty, intellectualism, or individualism (Withey 1965, Scott 1965, Bales & Couch 1969). Other scales tend to measure traits and occupational interests (Allport, Vernon & Lindzey 1960, Tagiuri 1965). These measures are inappropriate because of their emphasis on individual attitudes versus specific preferences for how organizations should run.

Organizational researchers have frequently used surrogate scales for the measurement of values. Such approaches include the measurement of values using the Protestant ethic (Kidron 1978), locals/cosmopolitans (Booth & Bisztray 1969) and Herzberg's intrinsic and extrinsic factors (Pennings 1970). These measures will not be considered because they suffer from the problems of inconsistent definition, and multiple conceptual and theoretical frameworks.

Pretest of Value Measure

The first scale developed to measure values was a Likert type scale of desirability. The instrument asked respondents to indicate the degree to which they felt each of twenty-one value statements was desirable for running a company. The seven point scale ranged from very undesirable to very desirable and provided a no opinion option. A pretest of this instrument was conducted on 49 business undergraduate students. Analysis of the responses revealed serious restriction of range. Discussion with subjects upon completion of the pretest supported the finding that all of the values were viewed as desirable. Table A-2 provides a breakdown of the frequencies of responses for the values used in the pretest. Over 85% of the respondents found seventeen of the twenty-one values to be desirable.

A value as defined in this study is a preferred state. The implication is that performance or desirability is a comparative or relative phenomena. Given the comparative nature of making preference statements and based on the pretest

Table A-1. Existing Measures of Values.

Interpersonal Values

    Survey of Interpersonal Values (Gordon 1960)
    Value Profile (Bales & Couch 1969)
    Dimensions of Values (Withey 1965)
    Faith in People (Rosenberg 1957)

Personal Values

    Personal Values Scales (Scott 1965)
    Study of Values (Allport, Vernon & Lindzey 1960)
    Test of Value Activities (Shorr 1953)
    Value Survey (Rokeach 1968)

Work Values

    Survey of Work Values (Wollack et al. 1971)
    Personal Values Questionnaire (England 1975)
    Occupational Values (Rosenberg 1957)
    Occupational Values Scales (Kilpatrick et al. 1964)
    Career-Oriented Occupational Values (Marvick 1954)

Moral Values

    Inventory of Values (Ewell 1954)
    Ways to Live (Morris 1956)
    Changes in Moral Values (Rettig & Pasamanick 1959)

Social Values

    Social Values Questionnaire (Perloe 1967)

---

finding of seeming desirability of most value statements, it seems logical to develop a measure of values that compares values one to another. In order to facilitate a *comparative* measure as opposed to a measure of *degree* of preference, a rank-order approach was taken. Respondents were asked to rank the five most and five least desirable values a company should have in running a business. The ranking format acknowledges that all the values are desirable, and focuses on prioritizing values.

    The final instrument developed for this study consists of twenty-four statements of organizational values. Five organizational goals utilized by England (1975) were adapted for use in this scale. England's scale has a history of use by organizational researchers (DeSalvia & Gemmill 1971, Watson & Simpson 1978, Schmidt & Posner 1982), and is consistent with the measurement criteria established for the study and the definition of values

Table A-2.   Value Statement Pretest.

VALUE STATEMENT	DESIRABILITY SCALE							
	VERY UNDESIRABLE	MODERATELY UNDESIRABLE	SLIGHTLY UNDESIRABLE	NEITHER DESIRABLE NOR UNDESIRABLE	SLIGHTLY DESIRABLE	MODERATELY DESIRABLE	VERY DESIRABLE	NO OPINION
High Productivity	0	0	0	2.0%	6.1%	40.8%	51.0%	0
Industry Leadership	0	0	2.0%	8.2%	16.3%	34.7%	38.8%	0
Employee Welfare	0	0	2.0%	0	12.2%	30.6%	55.1%	0
Superior Quality	0	0	0	4.1%	2.0%	10.2%	81.6%	2.0%
Company Stability	0	2.0%	0	6.1%	6.1%	26.5%	55.1%	4.1%
Social Well Being	0	2.0%	2.0%	6.1%	32.7%	30.6%	24.5%	0
Company Growth	0	0	0	10.2%	20.4%	32.7%	36.7%	0
Profit Maximization	0	0	2.0%	2.0%	20.4%	46.9%	28.6%	0
Low Turnover	0	2.0%	2.0%	8.2%	22.4%	30.6%	34.7%	0
High Morale	0	0	0	4.1%	8.2%	22.4%	65.3%	0
Employee Satisfaction	0	0	0	4.1%	14.3%	22.4%	59.2%	0
Survival	2.0%	0	0	6.1%	4.1%	12.2%	73.5%	2.0%
Adaptability	0	0	0	0	8.2%	30.6%	59.2%	2.0%
Creative Product Development	0	0	0	14.3%	34.7%	24.5%	24.5%	0
Reduced Labor Costs	0	2.0%	6.1%	12.2%	34.7%	30.6%	12.2%	2.0%
Open Communication	0	0	2.0%	4.1%	16.3%	34.7%	42.9%	0
Employee Development	0	0	2.0%	10.2%	18.4%	42.9%	26.5%	0
Growth In Sales	0	0	0	4.1%	16.3%	40.8%	36.7%	0
Employee Cohesiveness	0	0	2.0%	16.3%	32.7%	30.6%	18.4%	0
Control Over The Environment	2.0%	2.0%	6.1%	16.3%	34.7%	28.6%	6.1%	4.1%
Superior Service	0	0	0	6.1%	8.2%	24.5%	59.2%	2.0%

used. Eleven values were derived from the literature on organizational effectiveness and goals (see Steers 1977). Analysis of the preliminary interview findings provided for the addition of eight values mentioned frequently by interviewees. These items represent value statements grounded in the work environment. The importance of these values lies in their distinctiveness as contextually relevant preferences.

Additions and modifications to the list of value statements were made as a result of comments in the interviews and an analysis of the card sort. Table A-3 provides a summary of the sources of the value statements used in the survey. The value "growth in sales" was deleted from the survey because it overlapped company growth. Employee cohesiveness was consistently considered an irrelevant or overlapping value by interviewees and was excluded from the survey. Additional alterations were made to the a priori value statements in order to increase the applicability of the value list to the companies studied.

Table A-3.   Sources of Value Statements.*

England (1975)	Interviews	Organizational Effectiveness Literature
Efficiency+	Professionalism	Superior Quality & Service+
Industry Leadership	Co. Individuality	Support Failures
Company Stability	Community Involvement	Low Turnover
Social Well Being	Aggressiveness	Profits+
Company Growth	Ethics	Employee Satisfaction
	Creativity	Survival
	Reduced Labor Costs	Open Communication
	Creative Product Development	Control Over The Environment
		Adaptability
		Employee Development
		High Morale

*Two statements were deleted as a result of the interviews; Growth in sales, and Employee cohesiveness.
⁺Denotes value statements which were modified during the interviews.

Value Congruity

Value congruity is composed of two key components: (1) the degree of similarity between two groups on a value and (2) the degree of importance attached to the value. Congruity exists when a high degree of similarity exists between a department and top management on the set of values regarded as most important. Measures of both perceived and latent value congruity are discussed in detail in chapter 3; hence, they will be excluded from the discussion here.

Critical Contingencies

Hinings et al. (1974) found that coping with unknowns was the variable most critical to power and the best predictor of departmental power. In their study, it was found that departments who coped with critical problem areas or uncertainties would be the most powerful subunits in the organization.

To measure critical contingencies the organizations studied were examined to determine their unique unpredictable or critical problems. From the interviews, a list of ten critical problems found to be unpredictable were developed for each company. Unlike the list of unpredictable occurrences developed by Hinings et al. (1974) the lists presented in table A-4 include outputs and cultural and environmental factors as well as inputs.

Using a seven point scale ranging from does not control to controls completely, the respondents were asked to indicate the degree to which each department controls each of the ten problems for the company. A "don't know" response was also available. A composite score for each department was obtained by summing the scores for the various issues. Isolating the responses of top management and summing these scores constituted a composite score of the ability of each department to control critical contingencies from the perspective of top management. Other departments' perceptions of critical contingencies were obtained by excluding the responses of each department in evaluating their own department's control of critical contingencies.

In summary, three different perspectives were taken in examining critical contingencies: the perspective of each department, top management, and other departments. These different perspectives on critical contingencies were matched with the three perspectives on power to avoid the problems of self-report bias.

Power

In this study power was measured in two ways. An overall measure of power similar to that used by Perrow (1971) and Salancik and Pfeffer (1974) was used. The second measure examined departmental power with regard to various issues. This multi-issue approach to power is similar to that used by Hinings et al. (1974). The measure was used to distinguish power in various situations or contexts.

A multi-respondent approach to power was adopted to counteract the arguments that perceptual measures of power are biased (Clark 1968). Self-report bias is reduced by having three distinct groups of employees evaluate departmental power. Departmental employees evaluate their own department's power, other departmental employees evaluate each department's power, and top management evaluates each department's power.

Overall Power

An overall measure of power was obtained by asking, "In general how much influence do you feel the following departments have in your company?" A seven point scale ranging from no influence to a very great deal of influence

Table A-4.   List of Critical Problems.

CRITICAL PROBLEMS

Food King	Roboto
Problems of Determining Customer Needs	Problems Determining Customer Wants
Problems with Turnover	Problems in Product Quality or Reliability
Problems in Financial Stability	Problems in Financial Stability
Problems of Attracting Sound Franchisees	Problems of Customer Ignorance of the Product
Problems with Managing & Maintaining Growth	Problems with Long Range Planning
Problems of Name Recognition & Company Image	Problems of Company Image & Reputation
Problems of Attracting & Retaining Employees	Problems of Recruiting & Training
Problems of Staying A Step Ahead of the Competition (Innovative)	Problems of Staying Current on Technological Changes
Problems with Quality, Service, Cleanliness & Atmosphere	Problems of Competing with Other Companies
Problems of Increasing Profitability	Problems in Monitoring & Controlling Costs

was used. An additional response of don't know was provided. This measure captures an attribution of power that may be potential power or based on previous actions.

Multiple respondent views of overall power were obtained by asking employees to indicate their perceptions of their own department's overall influence and the influence of every other department. Top management was asked to indicate their perceptions of the influence of each department.

Issue-oriented Power

From the interviews, four unique power issues were identified for each company and six issues shared in common by both companies. A power issue was determined by the following criteria: a frequently mentioned facet of the organization or a recurrent problem area where more than one department is involved. This set of criteria is in keeping with the conceptualization of power issues stated by Hinings et al. (1974). Table A-5 lists the issues used to measure power in this study.

Power was measured using a seven point scale ranging from no ability to affect outcomes to greatest ability to affect outcomes. An additional scale item was included allowing the respondent to indicate that he or she does not know whether a department has the ability to affect the specific outcomes. Both potential and actual power are present in this issue-oriented measure of power.

As noted, three different respondent groups' measures of perceived power were used. One measure is the perception of one's own department. The individual scores of departmental personnel were averaged to arrive at this score. The score is a within department measure of power. To determine the perceptions other departments have of a particular department's power, the scores from each department's rating of a particular department, excluding the scores of the department being rated, were averaged. This constitutes a measure of department power based on the perceptions of members of other departments. The third measure of department power is the average power score for each department derived from top managers.

Composite scores for each department and top management were obtained by averaging all the scores for the various issues. The use of a composite measure may result in masking extreme differences concerning specific issues. On the other hand, the measure does capture the multi-dimensional aspects of power.

The Reliability and Validity of Measurement

Attempts to ascertain the reliability of the measures used in this study are hampered by the nature of the constructs investigated. All of the measures used examine more than one characteristic or factor of the designated variable. Because the measures contain more than one factor, all but one method for computing a reliability coefficient are inappropriate. Split-half reliability coefficients are obtainable for multifactor variables and provide a straightforward means of verifying the internal consistency of a measure (Ghiselli, Champbell & Zedeck 1981).

The perceived value congruity measures for each company were examined using Guttman's split-half reliability coefficient. For Food King, the measure of perceived value congruity with top management yielded a split-half reliability coefficient of .87 and the measure of congruity with the president had an internal consistency coefficient of .90. Perceived value congruity with top management and congruity with the president in Roboto yielded coefficients of .95 and .94 respectively. These split-half coefficients

Table A-5. List of Power Issues.

Food King	POWER ISSUES	Roboto
Major Capital Expenditures (Acquisitions of Stores)		Customer Satisfaction
Recruiting, Training & Employee Development		When Shipment of the Product will Occur
Quality, Service, Cleanliness & Atmosphere		Development of Policy & Policy Changes
Creation of a Unique Culture		Creation of a Unique Culture
Long Range Planning (Future Direction)		Long Range Planning (Future Direction)
Increase in Sales		Increases in Sales
Enhancement of a Company Reputation		Enhancement of a Company Reputation
Communication Between Departments		Communication Between Departments
Introduction of New Products		Introduction of New Products
Problems of Increasing Profitability		Problems in Monitoring & Controlling Costs

indicate that the measures of perceived value congruity have a high degree of internal consistency.

Tests of internal consistency were not considered appropriate for the other measures used in this study because the items developed are not intended to be homogeneous and the scores of multiple respondents are not separable. Unlike the measures of perceived value congruity that focused on a respondent's own department and twenty-four value statements, the measures of power and critical contingencies were based on the responses of multiple subunits and addressed unrelated issues within each instrument. Pretesting was not conducted on the critical contingencies and power measures because these instruments were designed to address the specific issues relevant to the organizations under study.

To improve the construct validity of the value measure interviewees were asked to judge the adequacy with which the list of value statements seemed to reflect the definition of the construct. Few additional value statements were suggested, but those suggested were incorporated into the survey measure. General agreement existed regarding the adequacy of the value statements in capturing all facets of organizational values. Numerous respondents remarked on the extensiveness of the list, noting that they could not think of any important values for running a business that were not included.

The construct validity of power was determined by a multitrait-multimethod approach (Campbell & Fiske 1959). Table A-6 provides the multitrait-multimethod matrix used to determine the relative contribution of trait and method variance. The three methods for measuring power were a department's own perceptions of its power, top management's perceptions of the department's power, and other departments' perceptions of the department's power.

Two traits were examined, issue based power and general power. Examination of the monotrait-heteromethod coefficients provides values ranging from .481 to .912. These values were significantly greater than zero, indicating evidence of convergent validity. That is, a high degree of association exists between issue-oriented power and the three different methods of measurement; and a high degree of association exists between general power and the three forms of measurement. The three requirements for discriminant validity identified by Campbell and Fiske (1959) were also met. The discriminant validity correlations were low, indicating that the two traits are different. In summary, the data presented in the matrix provides support for the presence of both convergent and discriminant validity in evaluating the measurement instruments for power.

Level of Analysis

The department was selected as the unit of analysis in this study because of its consistency with the purpose of the study. The purpose of this study is to examine the role of value congruity of a department and top management on departmental power. Clearly, the primary consideration in choosing a unit of analysis is the theoretical and research objective (see Haney 1980 for guidelines on how to choose a unit of analysis). The selection of the department as the unit of analysis is theoretically consistent with existing research on intraorganizational power and is also a meaningful and easily identifiable unit.

To arrive at departmental scores for each of the variables, the responses of department members were transferred into a department mean. In establishing department scores all respondents' scores were included and

Table A-6. Multitrait-Multimethod Matrix for Power.

TRAITS		METHODS*					
		M1		M2		M3	
		Issue A1	General B1	Issue A2	General B2	Issue A3	General B3
M1	A1						
	B1	.164					
M2	A2	.570	.437				
	B2	.253	.737	.605			
M3	A3	.481	.469	.912	.587		
	B3	.261	.717	.711	.892	.734	

*M1 = A department's perception of their own power
M2 = Top management's perception of a department's power
M3 = Other departments' perceptions of a department's power

equal weights were given to all individual responses. Using all of the respondents' scores was a conscious decision to avoid a common weakness of existing studies. Current research on departmental power relies exclusively on the perceptions of department heads. This practice has resulted in a clear managerial bias in the reporting of research pertaining to departmental power. Equal weights were given to all individual responses because a decision rule for variable weighting would be arbitrary.

Some argue that individual level data when aggregated becomes questionable to represent group variables. This problem appears to be serious when cross-level data are collected; that is, data collected at two levels of aggregation (Hannan 1971, Firebaugh 1980). In a recent test of aggregation bias it was found that aggregation of individual data led to insignificant bias in some cases and systematic bias in others, providing evidence for the acceptability of using individual data (Moorman 1979).

This study collects data from individual department members, asked to reflect on their department and other departments. The unit of analysis is the department, never the individual and no cross-level data was collected. Respondents were asked to focus on departmental not individual phenomenon; for example, to "focus on whether YOUR DEPARTMENT and

Top Management might share similar values" or "the degree to which each department has the ability to influence . . . ." Hannan (1971) argues that too much emphasis on aggregation problems may stifle research rather than improve research practice. In summary, the aggregation of individual scores to group means is based on the purpose of the research, precedence in similar research, and some evidence to suggest that aggregation bias is not a significant problem.

Appendix B

Interview Guide and Affect Checklist

Interview Guide

1. What are the three major problems a company encounters in the
    _____ industry?

    a. Which of these problems are most critical to the success of
        Roboto?

    b. How does Roboto deal with these critical problems? How
        should they?

    c. Which departments or groups of people are most involved or
        necessary in solving these problems.

2. What things are the most unpredictable in your industry, the things
    you lack information on.

    a. Which groups of people best deal with these unknowns (effectively
        manage/cope)?

    b. Which departments should deal with these unknowns?

    c. Which groups deal with the most unknowns? Least? Why?

3. If you could describe Roboto as an animal, what animal would you
    choose? What characteristics of that animal make it a good
    description?

4. What are the five most important things a company should value in
    running a business? I think a company should believe in _____.
    I think a company should act _____.

5. What are some of the things Roboto believes are important in running
    a company; what does Roboto stand for?

    a. Do you agree with these beliefs? Why?

    b. Are your values different?

    c. Is there a group of persons in Roboto whose beliefs or preferences for running a company most closely resemble yours? (see chart)

    d. Are most dissimilar to yours?

    e. Are you similar to top management?

6. I need your help in an activity designed to capture your preferences for some specific beliefs concerning how a company should be run. Sort these cards into piles. In one pile place the five most important values a company should have in running a business. In the second pile place the five least important values a company should have in running a business.

    a. If you were to sort them again considering the five most important values which Roboto has in running this company based on their actions, would the list be different from yours? How would it be different?

    b. Are there any important beliefs that should be added to this list?

7. How would you describe to a trusted friend what it's like working for Roboto. Assume that the person you are describing Roboto to knows nothing about Roboto.

    a. Are there any important things a person needs to know to succeed or survive at Roboto.

8. In many companies, a few groups or departments are able to affect the outcomes of many issues. Which groups at Roboto have the ability to affect the outcomes of other groups? Why? When?

    a. Are these groups generally influential or does it depend on the situation? Issue? If so, when are these groups influential?

    b. Which groups are least able to affect others?

    c. Which groups have the most influence with top management? Why? When? How do they use it?

9. What are the major strengths of Roboto? Weaknesses?

10. Generally speaking, are you satisfied working for Roboto?

    a. What would it take for you to leave the company?

Affect Checklist

DATE: _____

NAME: _____

POSITION: _____

LENGTH OF INTERVIEW: _____

----

1. In general, what was the respondent's attitude toward the interview?
    (Mark all that apply.)

    a. Friendly   b. Nervous
    c. Hostile   d. Uneasy
    e. Indifferent   f. Suspicious
    g. Open   h. Cautious
    i. Cooperative, but not particularly friendly
    j. Other   Specify _____

2. Were there any particular questions in the interview which the
    respondent had difficulty with? (YES   NO)

    Which question? _____

    _____

    Why? _____

3. Did the respondent understand the questions? (YES   NO)

    If no, what questions were not clear? _____

    _____

    Why? _____

4. Were there any unusual dynamics between the respondent and the
    interviewer during the session. (This includes interruptions,
    digressions, rapport, or fatigue of persons.)

    _____

    _____

Appendix C

Perceived Value Congruity Scale

Below are statements concerning several aspects of businesses. Each item states a belief regarding how a company should operate.

In this section, the focus is on whether your DEPARTMENT, and TOP MANAGEMENT might share similar values.

Top management is divided into two groups. In one group (I) is the president and Chief Executive Officer. In another group (II) are the highest ranking managers such as vice presidents or department heads.

Read each description and indicate the degree of similarity you believe exists between YOUR DEPARTMENT and the president. Next indicate the degree of similarity you believe exists between YOUR DEPARTMENT and the group of department heads known as top management.

1	2	3	4	5	6	7	8
VERY DISSIMILAR	MODERATELY DISSIMILAR	SLIGHTLY DISSIMILAR	NEITHER SIMILAR NOR DISSIMILAR	SLIGHTLY SIMILAR	MODERATELY SIMILAR	VERY SIMILAR	DON'T KNOW

INDICATE THE DEGREE OF SIMILARITY OF VALUES BETWEEN YOUR DEPARTMENT AND THE PRESIDENT. ALSO THE DEGREE OF SIMILARITY BETWEEN YOUR DEPARTMENT AND TOP MANAGEMENT.

	PRESIDENT I	TOP MGMT. II
1. Professionalism: Behaving in a business-like manner.		
2. Community Involvement: Concern for and active involvement in the community.		
3. Company Individuality: Being regarded by everyone in the industry as having a unique identity as a company.		
4. Aggressiveness: Being considered a bold, enterprising company. Actively hustling in the marketplace.		
5. Ethics: A company's concern for the honesty and integrity of all employees in conducting company activities.		
6. Creativity: Being imaginative and innovative in the development and delivery of the product and in handling business activities.		
7. Efficiency: Producing the product with minimal effort, waste and expense.		
8. Industry Leadership: Being considered by everyone in the industry to be the number one company (the best) in an industry.		
9. Superior Quality & Service: Making a good product and addressing all the needs of the customer as fast and friendly as possible.		
10. Support Failures: A willingness to support group or individual failures.		
11. Company Stability: Maintaining the existing operation over time.		
12. Social Well Being: A company's concern for the well-being of the community and society in general.		
13. Company Growth: An increase in various facets of a company, such as manpower, assets, sales, and market share.		
14. Profits: Making as much money as a company can.		
15. Low Turnover: A low number of people who willingly choose to leave a company.		
16. High Morale: A positive feeling for the company, a feeling of belonging.		
17. Employee Satisfaction: Feeling content about a job and the company. Having fun.		
18. Survival: Staying in business.		
19. Adaptability: The ability of a company to change its standard operating procedures in response to outside forces.		
20. Creative Product Development: The development of new and different products.		
21. Reduced Labor Costs: The ability to reduce the cost of employing workers.		
22. Open Communication: Ease of giving and getting information in an organization. The importance of informal communication across levels and departments.		
23. Employee Development: Expanding the skills and abilities of employees.		
24. Control Over the Environment: The ability to influence things which happen outside an organization that impact on what happens inside an organization.		

Appendix D

Research Hypotheses

Three research questions guide this investigation into the role of values. First, what is the influence of value congruity on departmental power? Second, what is the incremental variation in departmental power uniquely associated with value congruity when critical contingencies factors are present? Third, which approach to value congruity, perceived value congruity or latent value congruity, has a stronger relationship with department power? Seven hypotheses are presented in this appendix representing the three research hypotheses noted above. The presentation of the hypotheses are grouped according to the research question of interests.

Value Congruity and Power

The first question examines the relationship between value congruity and departmental power. It is hypothesized that sharing similar values with top management will increase the power of the congruent department relative to other departments.

Recognition of congruity of values may vary depending on whether the perceiver is top management or a department. How top management perceives its congruity with the various departments and how each department perceives its similarity with top management constitute the two viewpoints explored in the study of Roboto and Food King. It is expected that the relationship between departmental power and value congruity is similar, regardless of the group evaluating congruity.

Perceptions of power will be examined from the perspective of: (1) each department's appraisal of their own power, (2) other departments' appraisal of each department's power, and (3) top management's appraisal of each department's power. This multiple approach to power is adopted to avoid common method bias, and ascertain the degree of consistency that different groups have concerning department power (Enz 1985c). It is expected that a relationship between value congruity and power will exist regardless of the group whose perceptions of power are examined.

To the extent that each department, other departments, and top management are consistent in interpreting power relationships common perceptions may exist. In summary, it is hypothesized here that departments who view themselves as similar to top management perceive themselves as powerful and are perceived as powerful by other departments and top management.

Two distinct approaches to value congruity are presented in the present study. The first approach stresses perceptions from the perspectives of top management and each department. Perceived value congruity is investigated in two ways, by examining a department's awareness of the similarity of values between itself and top management, or top management's view of similarity with the department. This approach to congruity allows both a department and top management to interpret and define whether values are similar. Clearly this approach is intersubjective in that the groups interpret their own social situation and define similarity.

The other approach to congruity is latent value congruity. This view of value similarity is derived by obtaining the values of a department and top management independently and calculating statistically whether similarity exists. This orientation does not require awareness of similarity or conscious examination of the other groups' values.

The purpose of the first two hypotheses is to examine the relationship between perceived measures of value congruity and power. Similarity from the perspective of each department and from the perspective of top management will be considered separately. Three subhypotheses are developed to reflect the different perceptual measures of power (i.e., own department, other departments, top management).

A Department's View

The following hypothesis can be set forth regarding perceived value congruity and a department's own perception of its power.

> Hypothesis 1-a: The greater the degree of perceived congruity on values between the department and top management as perceived by the department, the greater the department's perceptions of their own power.

To determine if top management and other departments also regard value congruent departments as powerful two additional subhypotheses are included. This multi-respondent approach to power is utilized to reduce the potential biasing effects of the self-report based hypothesis.

> Hypothesis 1-b: The greater the degree of perceived congruity on values between the department and top management as perceived by the department, the greater top management's perceptions of the department's power.

Hypothesis 1-c: The greater the degree of perceived congruity on values between the department and top management as perceived by the department, the greater other departments' perceptions of the department's power.

Top Management's View

When top management believes that a department shares organizationally relevant values, it is hypothesized here that the department will be considered powerful in the eyes of top management, in its own perceptions and in the views of other department members. Top management's perceptions may be the most critical in determining the ability of a department to influence outcomes. The literature on top manager image suggests that the views of leaders significantly shape the attitudes and beliefs of other organizational participants.

Below are the hypotheses dealing with value congruity from the perspective of top management. Once again power is considered from the viewpoints of three different groups.

Hypothesis 2-a: The greater the degree of perceived congruity on values between the department and top management as perceived by top management, the greater the department's perceptions of their own power.

Hypothesis 2-b: The greater the degree of perceived congruity on values between the department and top management as perceived by top management, the greater top management's perceptions of the department's power.

Hypothesis 2-c: The greater the degree of perceived congruity on values between the department and top management as perceived by top management, the greater other departments' perceptions of the department's power.

Latent Value Congruity

In the everyday operation of a company, decisions are made on the basis of values that are not organizationally prescribed or recognized, but nevertheless influence the operation of the organization. Latent value congruity may determine power relationships that are unconscious, but have an impact on organizational functioning. Is awareness of value similarity necessary for a department to view itself as powerful? It is hypothesized here that power does not depend on an awareness of shared values. Influence occurs without conscious recognition of values. If a department is similar to top management in values, the department is powerful even if the department, other departments, or top management are not aware of the similarity. A department need not be aware of its similarity of values to be assessed as powerful.

As noted before, awareness of the fit of values is not necessary for congruity to be associated with power. In fact it is possible that the most congruent groups are not conscious of the similarity of values. Latent value congruity may direct behavior that currently escapes explanation. Numerous authors suggest that values guide actions and behaviors; thus, values may play a critical but indirect or disguised role in power relationships. Top managers may perceive departments that share values to be more like themselves, thus deserving of more power. In addition, top managers may unconsciously attach "rational" explanations to decisions based on value similarity. Hence, the following hypotheses are made:

Hypothesis 3-a: The greater the degree of latent congruity on values between the department and top management, the greater the department's own perceptions of power.

Hypothesis 3-b: The greater the degree of latent congruity on values between the department and top management, the greater top management's perceptions of the department's power.

Hypothesis 3-c: The greater the degree of latent congruity on values between the department and top management, the greater other departments' perceptions of the department's power.

The hypotheses developed up to this point all address the association between value congruity and departmental power. The next three hypotheses will consider the extent to which departmental power is associated with value congruity when the effects of critical contingencies are held constant.

Incremental Explanatory Power of Value Congruity

The second research question investigates whether value congruity provides any additional explanation of department power beyond that provided by critical contingencies. The interest in examining the unique predictive power of value congruity rests in challenging the critical contingencies literature. The present research question suggests that value congruity is another determinant of power.

The two perceptual measures of value congruity will be examined separately as in the two earlier hypotheses because they capture different perspectives on value congruity. It is hypothesized that the unique contribution of value congruity will be significant regardless of the group perceiving similarity.

Departmental Perceptions

The next three subhypotheses explore the degree to which value congruity as perceived by departments offers unique association with departmental power when critical contingencies are statistically controlled. As in the previous hypotheses, power is viewed by three different groups.

Hypothesis 4-a: The perceived value congruity between the department and top management, as perceived by the department, will account for significant variation in a department's perception of their own power beyond that provided by critical contingencies.

Hypothesis 4-b: The perceived value congruity between the department and top management, as perceived by the department, will account for significant variation in top management's perception of the department's power beyond that provided by critical contingencies.

Hypothesis 4-c: The perceived value congruity between the department and top management, as perceived by the department, will account for significant variation in other departments' perceptions of the department's power beyond that provided by critical contingencies.

Top Management's Perceptions

As suggested earlier, top management may perceive its value similarity with a department differently than a department would. Although the study predicts that the same relationships will exist regardless of who is perceiving similarity, it is necessary to treat these outlooks on values separately for purposes of hypothesis testing. Three hypotheses are developed for examining congruity as viewed by top management.

Hypothesis 5-a: The perceived value congruity between the department and top management, as perceived by top management, will account for significant variation in a department's perception of their own power beyond that provided by critical contingencies.

Hypothesis 5-b: The perceived value congruity between the department and top management, as perceived by top management, will account for significant variation in top management's perception of the department's power beyond that provided by critical contingencies.

Hypothesis 5-c: The perceived value congruity between the department and top management, as perceived by top management, will account for significant variation in other departments' perceptions of the department's power beyond that provided by critical contingencies.

Latent Value Congruity

The last set of hypotheses examine the incremental predictive power of value congruity focusing on similarity that is not consciously or explicitly known. Latent value congruity may be a better indicator of "true" value congruity, although it does not follow that this measure is a better predictor of power. The purpose behind examining the research question from this perspective is to offer a view of shared values that reduces the threats of misperception and social desirability.

> Hypothesis 6-a: Latent value congruity between the departments and top management will account for significant variation in a department's perceptions of their own power, beyond that provided by critical contingencies.

> Hypothesis 6-b: Latent value congruity between the departments and top management will account for significant variation in top management's perceptions of the department's power, beyond that provided by critical contingencies.

> Hypothesis 6-c: Latent value congruity between the departments and top management will account for significant variation in other departments' perceptions of the department's power, beyond that provided by critical contingencies.

Perceived versus Latent Value Congruity

Perceived value congruity and latent value congruity have been presented as two distinct facets of similarity. Which of these two aspects of congruity is most strongly associated with department power? It is hypothesized that perceived value congruity is more strongly associated with power than is latent value congruity. In cases of inconsistency between latent and perceived value congruity it is reasoned that perceived value congruity may prevail.

Perceived values focus on what is espoused and latent values capture the "true" preferences. A department may have different latent values than top management but espouse similar values in order to gain the trust or respect of the leaders. The link to power suggests that powerful departments may be those that are skilled at espousing the "right values" rather than actually sharing the same values.

In light of the arguments above, the following hypothesis is presented:

> Hypothesis 7: Perceived value congruity will be more strongly associated with power than latent value congruity, regardless of whether power is perceived by top management or a department.

This investigation into value congruity and power examines three questions: (1) "Is value congruity associated with departmental power?" (2) "Does value congruity provide any unique explanations of power?" and (3) "Which approach to congruity is most strongly related to power?" Each of the hypothesized relationships are concerned with exploring and refining the impact of different forms of value congruity on power. Chapter Four provides the results of a preliminary test of the seven hypotheses. See appendix E for the detailed quantitative findings that correspond to the hypotheses.

Appendix E

Research Findings

Table E-1. Hierarchical Regression of Perceived Value Congruity with Top Management as a Determinant of a Department's Own Power.

(N = 29)

REGRESSION EQUATIONS	REGRESSION EQUATION IN FINAL STEP			HIERARCHICAL REGRESSION CORRELATION COEFFICIENTS	
	Standardized Regression Coefficients	Partial F tests	Overall F tests	Multiple R^2	Change in Multiple R^2
ISSUE ORIENTED POWER					
Critical Contingencies[+] Value Congruity with Top Management	.632	----	23.613****	.476	.476
	.211	2.122	13.377****	.517	.041
Critical Contingencies Value Congruity with President	.450	----	11.946***	.307	.307
	.393	6.809**	10.673****	.451	.144
GENERAL POWER					
Critical Contingencies Value Congruity with Top Management	.282	----	8.830***	.247	.247
	.640	27.602****	17.880****	.589	.342
Critical Contingencies Value Congruity with President	.427	----	8.834***	.247	.247
	.265	2.473	5.894***	.312	.065

[+]Critical contingencies are derived from each department's perceptions of their own department.

*p < .10
**p < .05
***p < .01
****p < .001

Table E-2. Hierarchical Regression of Perceived Value Congruity with
Top Management as a Determinant of Power as Perceived
by Top Management.
(N = 29)

REGRESSION EQUATIONS	REGRESSION EQUATION IN FINAL STEP			HIERARCHICAL REGRESSION CORRELATION COEFFICIENTS	
	Standardized Regression Coefficients	Partial F tests	Overall F tests	Multiple R^2	Change in Multiple R^2
ISSUE ORIENTED POWER					
Critical Contingencies[+] Value Congruity with Top Management	.882	----	86.813****	.770	.770
Value Congruity with President	-.013	.016	41.772****	.770	.0002
Critical Contingencies Value Congruity with President	.857	----	79.261****	.746	.746
	.023	.047	38.254****	.746	.0005
GENERAL POWER					
Critical Contingencies Value Congruity with Top Management	.511	----	15.686****	.376	.376
	.278	2.998*	9.944****	.443	.067
Critical Contingencies Value Congruity with President	.618	----	18.090****	.401	.401
	.048	.092	8.786****	.403	.002

[+]Critical contingencies are derived from top management's perceptions of each department.

*p < .10
**p < .05
***p < .01
****p < .001

Table E-3. Hierarchical Regression of Perceived Value Congruity with Top Management as a Determinant of Power as Perceived by Other Departments.

(N = 29)

REGRESSION EQUATIONS	REGRESSION EQUATION IN FINAL STEP			HIERARCHICAL REGRESSION CORRELATION COEFFICIENTS	
	Standardized Regression Coefficients	Partial F tests	Overall F tests	Multiple R^2	Change in Multiple R^2
ISSUE ORIENTED POWER					
Critical Contingencies[+]	.909	----	110.787****	.810	.810
Value Congruity with Top Management	-.036	.163	53.692****	.811	.001
Critical Contingencies	.907	----	115.103****	.810	.810
Value Congruity with President	-.049	.321	56.270****	.812	.002
GENERAL POWER					
Critical Contingencies	.566	----	17.124****	.397	.397
Value Congruity with Top Management	.264	3.034*	10.750****	.462	.065
Critical Contingencies	.650	----	21.374****	.442	.442
Value Congruity with President	.094	.410	10.654****	.450	.009

[+]Critical contingencies are derived from other departments' perceptions of each department.

*$p < .10$
**$p < .05$
***$p < .01$
****$p < .001$

Table E-4. Hierarchical Regression of Perceived Value Congruity with Departments as a Determinant of a Department's Own Power.
(N = 29)

REGRESSION EQUATIONS	REGRESSION EQUATION IN FINAL STEP			HIERARCHICAL REGRESSION CORRELATION COEFFICIENTS	
	Standardized Regression Coefficients	Partial F tests	Overall F tests	Multiple R^2	Change in Multiple R^2
Power from the perspective of each department					
ISSUE-ORIENTED POWER					
Critical Contingencies[+]	.298	----	2.929	.087	.087
Value Congruity with each department	.332	4.451**	3.849**	.228	.142
GENERAL POWER					
Critical Contingencies	.528	----	12.787****	.321	.321
Value Congruity with each department	.262	2.852*	8.258***	.388	.067

[+]Critical contingencies are derived from each department's perceptions of their own department.

*p < .10
**p < .05
***p < .01
****p < .001

Table E-5. Hierarchical Regression of Perceived Value Congruity with
Departments as a Determinant of Power as Perceived
by Top Management.
(N = 29)

| | REGRESSION EQUATION IN FINAL STEP | | | HIERARCHICAL REGRESSION CORRELATION COEFFICIENTS | |
REGRESSION EQUATIONS	Standardized Regression Coefficients	Partial F tests	Overall F tests	Multiple R^2	Change in Multiple R^2
Power from the perspective of top management					
ISSUE ORIENTED POWER					
Critical Contingencies[+]	.829	----	79.261***	.746	.746
Value Congruity with each department	.231	6.685**	51.317***	.798	.052
GENERAL POWER					
Critical Contingencies	.566	----	18.090****	.402	.402
Value Congruity with each department	.454	13.232****	19.759****	.603	.202

[+]Critical contingencies are derived from top management's perspective of each department.

*p < .10
**p < .05
***p < .01
****p < .001

Table E-6. Hierarchical Regression of Perceived Value Congruity with
Departments as a Determinant of Power as Perceived
by Other Departments.
(N = 29)

| | REGRESSION EQUATION IN FINAL STEP | | | HIERARCHICAL REGRESSION CORRELATION COEFFICIENTS | |
REGRESSION EQUATIONS	Standardized Regression Coefficients	Partial F tests	Overall F tests	Multiple R^2	Change in Multiple R^2
Power from the perspective of other departments					
ISSUE ORIENTED POWER					
Critical Contingencies+	.829	----	74.285****	.733	.733
Value Congruity with each department	.184	3.707*	42.719****	.767	.033
GENERAL POWER					
Critical Contingencies	.638	----	24.463****	.475	.475
Value Congruity with each department	.347	7.532***	18.957****	.593	.118

+Critical contingencies are derived from other departments' perceptions of each department.

*p < .10

**p < .05

***p < .01

****p < .001

Table E-7. Hierarchical Regression of Latent Value Congruity as a Determinant of Power as Perceived by Own Department.

(N = 29)

REGRESSION EQUATIONS	REGRESSION EQUATION IN FINAL STEP			HIERARCHICAL REGRESSION CORRELATION COEFFICIENTS	
	Standardized Regression Coefficients	Partial F tests	Overall F tests	Multiple R^2	Change in Multiple R^2
ISSUE ORIENTED POWER					
OVERALL VALUE CONGRUITY Critical Contingencies	.677	----	11.964**	.307	.307
Value Congruity on values ranked #1	-.557	19.305***	19.690***	.602	.295
Critical Contingencies	.529	----	11.964**	.308	.308
Value Congruity on values ranked #2	.091	.293	5.972**	.315	.008
MOST IMPORTANT VALUES Critical Contingencies	.614	----	11.964**	.307	.307
Value Congruity on values ranked #1	-.127	.508	6.127**	.320	.013
Critical Contingencies	.620	----	16.680***	.391	.391
Value Congruity on values ranked #2	.030	.036	8.049**	.392	.0008
GENERAL POWER					
OVERALL VALUE CONGRUITY Critical Contingencies	.469	----	8.834**	.247	.247
Value Congruity on values ranked #1	.127	.536	4.609*	.262	.015
Critical Contingencies	.562	----	8.834**	.247	.247
Value Congruity on values ranked #2	-.238	1.938	5.539**	.299	.002
MOST IMPORTANT VALUES Critical Contingencies	.494	----	8.834**	.247	.247
Value Congruity on values ranked #1	.000	.001	4.254*	.247	.001
Critical Contingencies	.528	----	9.726**	.272	.272
Value Congruity on values ranked #2	-.037	.046	4.707*	.274	.002

*p < .10
**p < .05
***p < .01
****p < .001

Table E-8. Hierarchical Regression of Latent Value Congruity as a Determinant of Power as Perceived by Top Management.
(N = 29)

REGRESSION EQUATIONS	REGRESSION EQUATION IN FINAL STEP			HIERARCHICAL REGRESSION CORRELATION COEFFICIENTS	
	Standardized Regression Coefficients	Partial F tests	Overall F tests	Multiple R^2	Change in Multiple R^2
ISSUES ORIENTED POWER					
OVERALL VALUE CONGRUITY					
Critical Contingencies	.906	----	79.261****	.746	.746
Value Congruity on					
values ranked #1	-.181	3.607*	45.259****	.777	.031
Critical Contingencies	.863	----	79.261****	.746	.746
Value Congruity on					
values ranked #2	.019	.035	38.232****	.747	.0003
MOST IMPORTANT VALUES					
Critical Contingencies	.873	----	79.261****	.746	.746
Value Congruity on					
values ranked #1	-.025	.054	38.270****	.746	.0005
Critical Contingencies	.863	----	76.334****	.746	.746
Value Congruity on					
values ranked #2	.094	.909	38.488****	.755	.009
GENERAL POWER					
OVERALL VALUE CONGRUITY					
Critical Contingencies	.618	----	18.090****	.401	.401
Value Congruity on					
values ranked #1	.066	.180	8.860****	.405	.004
Critical Contingencies	.634	----	18.090****	.401	.401
Value Congruity on					
values ranked #2	-.054	.127	8.816****	.404	.003
MOST IMPORTANT VALUES					
Critical Contingencies	.590	----	18.090****	.401	.401
Value Congruity on					
values ranked #1	.122	.578	9.192****	.414	.013
Critical Contingencies	.633	----	17.356****	.400	.4000
Value Congruity on					
values ranked #2	.042	.075	8.410***	.402	.002

*p < .10
**p < .05
***p < .01
****p < .001

Hierarchical Regression of Latent Value Congruity as a
Determinant of Power as Perceived by Other Departments.
$(N = 29)$

REGRESSION EQUATIONS	REGRESSION EQUATION IN FINAL STEP			HIERARCHICAL REGRESSION CORRELATION COEFFICIENTS	
	Standardized Regression Coefficients	Partial F tests	Overall F tests	Multiple R^2	Change in Multiple R^2
ISSUE ORIENTED POWER					
OVERALL VALUE CONGRUITY					
Critical Contingencies	.935	----	115.103****	.810	.810
Value Congruity on					
values ranked #1	.107	1.470	59.287****	.820	.010
Critical Contingencies	.906	----	115.103****	.810	.810
Value Congruity on					
values ranked #2	-.039	.202	55.950****	.812	.002
MOST IMPORTANT VALUES					
Critical Contingencies	.945	----	115.103****	.810	.810
Value Congruity on					
values ranked #1	-.108	1.401	59.107****	.820	.010
Critical Contingencies	.904	----	110.943****	.810	.810
Value Congruity on					
values ranked #2	-.026	.086	53.565****	.810	.0007
GENERAL POWER					
OVERALL VALUE CONGRUITY					
Critical Contingencies	.656	----	21.374****	.442	.442
Value Congruity on					
values ranked #1	.026	.027	10.320****	.442	.0006
Critical Contingencies	.691	----	21.374****	.442	.442
Value Congruity on					
values ranked #2	-.165	1.290	11.446****	.468	.026
MOST IMPORTANT VALUES					
Critical Contingencies	.634	----	21.374****	.442	.442
Value Congruity on					
values ranked #1	.073	.206	10.475****	.446	.004
Critical Contingencies	.667	----	20.915****	.446	.446
Value Congruity on					
values ranked #2	.000	.001	10.056****	.446	.00003

*p < .10
**p < .05
***p < .01
****p < .001

Bibliography

Abravanel, H. "Mediatory Myths in the Service of Organizational Ideology." In L. Pondy, P. Frost, G. Morgan, and T. Dandridge, *Organizational Behavior and Industrial Relations* (Monographs in *Organizational Symbolism,* vol. 1), 273–93. Greenwich, CT: JAI Press, 1983.

Adler, F. "The Value Concept in Sociology." *The American Journal of Sociology* 62 (1956–57): 272–79.

Alderfer, C.P. and Brown, L.D. "Designing an 'Empathic Questionnaire' for Organizational Research." *Journal of Applied Psychology* 56, no. 6 (1972): 456–60.

Allen, R.F. "Four Phases for Bringing about Cultural Change." In R.H. Kilmann, M.J. Saxton, R. Serpa, and associates (eds.), *Gaining Control of the Corporate Culture,* 332–50. San Francisco: Jossey-Bass Inc., 1985.

Allport, G.W. *Pattern and Growth in Personality.* New York: Holt, Rinehart, & Winston, 1961.

Allport, G.W.; Vernon, P.E.; and Lindzey, G. *A Study of Values.* Boston: Houghton Mifflin, 1960.

Andrews, K.R. *The Concept of Corporate Strategy.* Homewood, IL: Richard D. Irvin Co., 1980.

Bacharach, S.B. and Aiken, M. "Structural and Process Constraints on Influence in Organizations: A Level Specific Analysis." *Administrative Science Quarterly* 21, no. 4 (1976): 623–42.

Bacharach, S.B. and Lawler, E.J. *Power and Politics in Organizations.* San Francisco: Jossey-Bass Inc., 1980.

Bagozzi, R. and Phillips, L. "Representing and Testing Organizational Theories: A Holistic Construal." *Administrative Science Quarterly* 27, no. 3 (1982): 459–89.

Baldridge, J.V. *Power and Conflict in the University.* New York: John Wiley & Sons, 1971.

Bales, R. and Couch, A. "The Value Profile: A Factor Analytic Study of Value Statements." *Sociological Inquiry* 39 (1969): 3–17.

Barley, S.R. "Semiotics and the Study of Occupational and Organizational Culture." *Administrative Science Quarterly* 28, no. 3 (1983): 393–413.

Barnard, C.I. *The Functions of the Executive.* Cambridge: Harvard University Press, 1938.

Becker, H.S. and Greer, B. "Latent Culture: A Note on the Theory of Latent Social Roles." *Administrative Science Quarterly* 5 (1960): 304–13.

Beyer, J.M. "Ideologies, values, and decision making in organizations." In Paul C. Nystrom and William H. Starbuck (eds.), *Handbook of Organizational Design,* vol. 2, 166–202. New York: Oxford University Press, 1981.

———. "Power Dependencies and the Distribution of Influence in Universities." In Samuel B. Bacharach (ed.), *Research in the Sociology of Organizations,* vol. 1, 167–208. Greenwich, CT: JAI Press, 1982.

Bidwell, C.E. and Kasarda, J.D. "Problems of Multilevel Measurement: The Case of School and Schooling." In K. Roberts and L. Burstein (eds.), *New Directions for Methodology of Social and Behavioral Science Issues in Aggregation,* 53–64. San Francisco: Jossey-Bass, 1980.

Blau, P.M., *Exchange and Power in Social Life.* New York: John Wiley & Sons, 1967.

Blumer, H. *Symbolic Interactionism: Perspective and Method.* Englewood Cliffs, NJ: Prentice-Hall, 1969.

Booth, A. and Bisztray, G. "Value Orientations, Member Integration and Participation in Voluntary Association Activities." *Administrative Science Quarterly* (1969): 39–45.

Bourgeois, L.J. "Performance and Consensus." *Strategic Management Journal* 1 (1980): 227–48.

Broder, D. "With Reagan, Information Can't Shake Ideology," *Courier-Journal* (Sept. 2, 1985).

Brown, M.A. "Values—A Necessary but Neglected Ingredient of Motivation on the Job." *Academy of Management Review* 1, (1976): 15–23.

Burger, P. and Luckmann, T. *The Social Construction of Reality.* New York: Doubleday, 1967.

Burrell, G. and Morgan, G. *Sociological Paradigms and Organizational Analysis.* London: Heinemann, 1979.

Campbell, D.T. and Fiske, D.W. "Convergent and Discriminant Validation by the Multitrait-Multimethod Matrix." *Psychological Bulletin* 56, no. 2 (1959): 81–105.

Carper, W.B. and Litschert, R.J. "Strategic Power Relationships in Contemporary Profit and Non-profit Hospitals." *Academy of Management Journal* 26 (1983): 311–20.

Carroll, D.T. "A Disappointing Search for Excellence." *Harvard Business Review* (Nov.-Dec. 1983): 78-88.

Cartwright, D. "Influence, Leadership, Control." In J. March (ed.), *Handbook of Organizations,* 1–47. Chicago: Rand McNally & Co., 1965.

Child, J. "Organizational Structure, Environment, and Performance: The Role of Strategic Choice." *Sociology* 6 (1972): 2–22.

Cicourel, A.V. *Method and Measurement in Sociology.* Glencoe, IL: Free Press, 1964.

Clark, B.R. *The Distinctive College: Antioch, Reed, and Swarthmore.* Chicago: Aldine, 1970.

———. "The Organizational Saga in Higher Education." *Administrative Science Quarterly* 17 (1972): 178–84.

Clegg, S. *Power, Rule and Domination.* Boston: Routledge & Kegan Paul, 1975.

———. "Power, Organization theory, Marx, and Critique." In S. Clegg and D. Dunkerley (eds.), *Critical Issues in Organizations.* Boston: Routledge & Kegan Paul, 1977.

Cohen, J. and Cohen, P. *Applied Multiple Regression/Correlation Analysis for the Behavioral Sciences.* New York: John Wiley & Sons, 1975.

Comstock, D.E. "Power In Organizations Toward a Critical Theory." *Pacific Sociological Review* 25, no. 2 (1982): 139–62.

Connor, P.E. and Becker, B.W. "Values and the Organization: Suggestions for Research." *Academy of Management Journal* (1975): 550–61.

Crittenden, K.S. and Hill, R.J. "Coding Reliability and Validity of Interview Data." *American Sociological Review* 36 (Dec. 1971): 1073–80.

Cronback, L.J. and Gleser, G.C. "Assessing Similarity Between Profiles." *The Psychological Bulletin* 50, no. 6 (1953): 456–73.

Crozier, M. *The Bureaucratic Phenomenon.* Chicago: University of Chicago Press, 1964.

Cyert, R.M. and March, J.G. *A Behavioral Theory of the Firm.* Englewood Cliffs, NJ: Prentice-Hall, 1963.

Daft, R.L. "System Influence on Organization Decision-Making: The Case of Resource Allocation." *Academy of Management Journal* 21 (1978): 6–22.

Dahl, R.A. "The Concept of Power." *Behavioral Science* 2 (1957): 201–15.

Dandridge, T.C.; Mitroff, I.; and Joyce, W. "Organizational Symbolism: A Topic to Expand Organizational Analysis." *Academy of Management Review* 5, no. 1 (1980).

Deal, T.E. and Kennedy, A.A. *Corporate Cultures: The Rites and Rituals of Corporate Life.* Reading, MA: Addison-Wesley, 1982.

DeSalvia, D.N. and Gemmill, G.R. "An Exploratory Study of the Personal Value Systems of College Students and Managers." *Academy of Management Journal* 14 (1971): 227–38.

Dowling, J. and Pfeffer, J. "Organizational Legitimacy: Social Values and Organizational Behavior." *Pacific Sociological Review* 18 (1975): 122–36.

Dubin, R. "Management: Meanings, Methods, and Moxie." *Academy of Management Review* 7, no. 3 (1982): 372–79.

Emerson, R.M. "Power-Dependence Relations." *American Sociological Review* 27 (1962): 31–41.

England, G.W. "Personal Value Systems of American Managers." *Academy of Management Journal* 10 (1967): 53–68.

_____. *The Manager and His Values: An International Perspective.* Cambridge, MA: Ballinger Publishing Company, 1975.

England, G.W. and Lee, R. "The Relationship Between Managerial Values and Managerial Success in the United States, Japan, India, and Australia." *Journal of Applied Psychology* 59, no. 4 (1974): 411–19.

Enz, C.A. *Perceived and Latent Value Congruity as Determinants of Intraorganizational Power.* Unpublished doctoral dissertation, Ohio State University, OH, 1985a.

_____. "New Directions for Cross-Cultural Studies: Linking Organizational and Societal Cultures." In R. Farmer (ed.), *Advances in International Comparative Management*, vol. 2. Greenwich, CT: JAI Press, 1985b, (Forthcoming).

_____. *The Measurement of Perceived Intraorganizational Power: A Multi-Respondent Perspective.* Unpublished manuscript, 1985c.

Epstein, E.M. *The Corporation in American Politics.* Englewood Cliffs, NJ: Prentice-Hall, 1969.

Etzioni, A. *A Comparative Analysis of Complex Organizations.* New York: The Free Press, 1961.

Evered, R. "The Language of Organizations: The Case of the Navy." In L. Pondy, P. Frost, G. Morgan, and T. Dandridge, *Organizational Behavior and Industrial Relations* (Monographs in Organizational Symbolism, vol. 1), 125–44. Greenwich, CT: JAI Press, 1983.

Ewell, A.H., Jr. Inventory in "The Relationship Between the Rigidity of Moral Values and the Severity of Functional Psychological Illness: A Study With War Veterans of One Religious Group." Doctoral dissertation, New York University, 1954.

Festinger, L.; Pepitone, A.; and Newcomb, T. "Some Consequences of Deindividuation in a Group." *Journal of Abnormal and Social Psychology* 47 (1952): 382–89.

Fine, G.A. "Small Groups and Culture Creation: The Idioculture of Little League Baseball Teams." *American Sociological Review* 44 (1979): 733–45.

Fine, G.A. and Kleinman, S. "Rethinking Subculture: An Interactionist Analysis." *American Journal of Sociology* 85 (1979): 1–20.

Firebaugh, G. "Groups as Contexts and Frog Ponds." In K. Roberts and L. Burstein (eds.), *New Directions for Methodology of Social and Behavioral Science* (vol. 6), 43–52. San Francisco: Jossey-Bass Inc., 1980.

French, J.R., and Raven, B. "The Bases of Social Power." In D. Cartwright (ed.), *Studies In Social Power*, 150–67. Ann Arbor: University of Michigan, Institute of Social Research, 1959.

Games, P.A. and Lucas, P.A. "Power of the Analysis of Variance of Independent Groups on Non-Normal and Normally Transformed Data." *Educational and Psychological Measurement* 26, no. 2 (1966): 311–27.

Geertz, C. *The Interpretation of Cultures.* New York: Basic Books Inc., 1973.

Ghiselli, E.; Campbell, J.; and Zedeck, S. *Measurement Theory for the Behavioral Sciences.* San Francisco: W.H. Freeman and Co., 1981.

Gordon, L. *Survey of Interpersonal Values.* Chicago: Science Research Associates, 1960.

Gregory, K.L. "Native-View Paradigms: Multiple Cultures and Culture Conflicts in Organizations." *Administrative Science Quarterly* 28, no. 3 (1983): 359–76.

Hage, J. and Dewar, R. "Elite Values versus Organizational Structure in Predicting Innovation." *Administrative Science Quarterly* 18 (1973): 279–90.

Hambrick, D.C. "Operationalizing the Concept of Business-Level Strategy in Research." *The Academy of Management Review* 5, no. 4 (1980): 567–76.

————. "Environment, Strategy, and Power Within Top Management Teams." *Administrative Science Quarterly* 26 (1981): 253–75.

Hambrick, D.C. and Mason, P.A. "Upper Echelons: The Organization as a Reflection of Its Top Managers." *Academy of Management Review* 9, no. 2 (1984): 193–206.

Haney, W. "Units and Levels of Analysis in Large-Scale Analysis." In K. Roberts and L. Burstein (eds.), *New Directions for Methodology of Social and Behavioral Science* (vol. 6), 1–16. San Francisco: Jossey-Bass Inc., 1980.

Hannan, M.T. *Aggregation and Disaggregation in Sociology.* Lexington, MA: Lexington Books, 1971.

Helsel, A.R. "Value Orientation and Pupil Control Ideology of Public School Educators." *Educational Administration Quarterly* 7 (1971): 24–33.

Hickman, C.R. and Silva, M.A. *Creating Excellence: Managing Corporate Culture, Strategy, and Change in the New Age.* New York: New American Library, 1984.

Hickson, D.J.; Hinings, C.R.; Lee, C.A.; Schneck, R.E.; and Pennings, J.M. "A Strategic Contingencies Theory of Intraorganizational Power." *Administrative Science Quarterly* 16, no. 2 (1971): 216–29.

Hillard, A.L. *The Forms of Value: The Extension of a Hedonistic Axiology.* New York: Columbia University Press, 1950.

Hills, F.S. and Mahoney, T.A. "University Budgets and Organizational Decision Making." *Administrative Science Quarterly* 23 (1978): 454–64.

Hinings, C.R.; Hickson, D.J.; Pennings, J.M.; and Schneck, R.E. "Structural Conditions of Intraorganizational Power." *Administrative Science Quarterly* 19 (1974): 22–44.

Hofstede, G. *Culture's Consequences: International Differences in Work-Related Values.* Beverly Hills: Sage Publications Inc., 1984.

Hollander, M. and Wolfe, D. *Nonparametric Statistical Methods.* New York: John Wiley & Sons, 1972.

Janis, I.L. *Victims of Groupthink.* Boston: Houghton Mifflin, 1972.

Johns, G. "Difference Score Measures of Organizational Behavior Variables: A Critique." *Organizational Behavior and Human Performance* 27 (1981): 443–63.

Kalberg, S. "Max Weber's Types of Rationality." *American Journal of Sociology* 85 (1980): 1145–79.

Kamens, D.H. "Legitimating Myths and Educational Organization: The Relationship Between Organizational Ideology and Formal Structure." *American Sociological Review* 42 (1977): 208–19.

Kaplan, A. "Power in Perspective." In R.L. Kahn and E. Boulding (eds.), *Power and Conflict in Organizations,* 11–32. London: Tavistock, 1964.

Kaufman, H. and Jones, V. "The Mystery of Power." *Public Administrative Review* 14 (1954): 204–15.

Kelman, H.C. "Compliance, Identification, and Internalization: The Processes of Attitude Change." *Journal of Conflict Resolution* 2 (1958): 51–60.

————. "Further Thoughts on the Process of Compliance, Identification, and Internalization." In J.T. Tedeschi (ed.), *Perspectives in Social Power.* Chicago: Aldine, 1974.

Kerlinger, F.N. *Foundations of Behavioral Research.* New York: Holt, Rinehart, and Winston, Inc., 1973.

Kidron, A. "Work Values and Organizational Commitment." *Academy of Management Journal* 21, no. 2 (1978): 239–47.

Kilmann, R.H. "Getting Control of the Corporate Culture." *Managing* 3 (1982): 11–17.

Kilpatrick, F.P.; Cummings, M.C.; and Jennings, M.K. *The Image of the Federal Service.* Washington, DC: The Brookings Institution, 1964.

Kipnis, D. *The Powerholders.* Chicago: University of Chicago Press, 1976.

Kluckholn, C. "Toward a Comparison of Value-Emphases in Different Cultures." In L.D. White (ed.), *The State of the Social Sciences.* Chicago, IL: University of Chicago Press, 1956.

_____. "The Study of Values." In D.N. Barrett, *Values in America.* Notre Dame, IN: University of Notre Dame Press, 1961.

_____. "Values and Value-Orientations in the Theory of Action." In Talcott Parsons and Edward A. Shils (eds.), *Toward a General Theory of Action,* 388–433. New York: Harper and Row, 1967.

Lawrence, P.R. and Lorsch, J.W. *Organization and Environment.* Homewood, IL: Richard D. Irwin Inc., 1967.

Lieberson, S. "Rank-Sum Comparisons Between Groups." In David R. Heise (ed.), *Sociological Methodology.* San Francisco: Jossey-Bass Inc., 1976.

Lodahl, J.B. and Gordon, G. "The Structure of Scientific Fields and the Functioning of University Graduate Departments." *American Sociological Review* 37 (1972): 57–72.

Lorange, P. *Corporate Planning.* Englewood Cliffs, NJ: Prentice-Hall, 1980.

Louis, M.R. "A Cultural Perspective on Organizations: The Need for and Consequences of Viewing Organizations as Culture-bearing Milieux." *Human Systems Management* 2 (1981): 246–58.

_____. "Organizations As Cultural-bearing Milieux." In L. Pondy, P. Frost, G. Morgan, and T. Dandridge, *Organizational Behavior and Industrial Relations* (Monographs in *Organizational Symbolism,* vol. 1), 39–54. Greenwich, CT: JAI Press, 1983.

Mannheim, K. *Ideology and Utopia.* (L. Wirth & E. Shils, trans.). New York: Harcourt Brace Jovanovich Inc., 1936.

March, J.G. "An Introduction to the Theory and Measurement of Influence." *American Political Science Review* 49 (1955): 431–51.

March, J.G. and Simon, H.A. *Organizations.* New York: John Wiley & Sons, 1958.

Martin, H.J. "Managing Specialized Corporate Cultures." In R.H. Kilmann, M.J. Saxton, R. Serpa and Assoc. (eds.), *Gaining Control of the Corporate Culture,* 148–62. San Francisco: Jossey-Bass, 1985.

Marvick, D. "Career Perspectives in a Bureaucratic Setting." (Michigan Government Studies, No. 27). Ann Arbor, MI: University of Michigan Press, 1954.

Mechanic, D. "Sources of Power of Lower Participants in Complex Organizations." *Administrative Science Quarterly* 7 (1962): 347–64.

Meyer, A.D. "How Ideologies Supplant Formal Structures and Shape Responses to Environments." *Journal of Management Studies* 19, no. 1 (1982): 45–61.

Meyer, J.W. and Rowan, B. "Institutionalized Organizations: Formal Structure as Myth and Ceremony." *American Journal of Sociology* 83, no. 2 (1977): 340–63.

Meyers, J.L. *Fundamentals of Experimental Design.* 3d ed. Boston: Allyn & Bacon Inc., 1979.

Miller, L.M. *American Spirit Visions of a New Corporate Culture.* New York: William Morrow and Co. Inc., 1984.

Mills, C.W. *Power Politics & People.* Irving Louis Horowitz (ed.). London: Oxford University Press, 1972.

Mintzberg, H. *Power in and around Organizations.* Englewood Cliffs, NJ: Prentice-Hall, 1983.

Moorman, J. "Aggregation Bias: An Empirical Demonstration." *Sociological Methods and Research* 8, no. 1 (1979): 69–94.

Morgan, G. "Paradigms, Metaphors and Puzzle Solving in Organization Theory." *Administrative Science Quarterly* 25 (1980): 605–22.

Morris, C. *Varieties of Human Value.* Chicago: University of Chicago Press, 1956.

Neter, J. and Wasserman, W. *Applied Linear Statistical Models.* Homewood, IL: Richard D. Irvin Inc., 1974.

Newcomb, T.M. "An Approach to the Study of Communicative Acts." *Psychological Review* 60, no. 6 (1953): 393–404.

Nuttall, K.R. *The Changing of Power In A Solar Energy Sales Company.* Unpublished paper, 1985.

Osgood, C.E.; Suci, G.J.; and Tannenbaum, R.H. *The Measurement of Meaning.* Chicago: University of Chicago Press, 1957.

Parsons, T. *The Structure of Social Action.* Glencoe, IL: Free Press, 1949.

———. *Structure and Process in Modern Societies.* New York: Free Press, 1960.

———. *The Social System.* New York: Free Press, 1964.

Parsons, T. and Shils, E.A. "Systems of Value-Orientation." In T. Parsons and E.A. Shils (eds.), *Toward a General Theory of Action.* Cambridge: Harvard University Press, 1967.

Pennings, J.M. "Work-Value Systems of White-Collar Workers." *Administrative Science Quarterly* 15 (1970): 397–405.

Perloe, S.I. "Social Values Questionnaire." Final report to Office of Education on Project S-308, Bureau No. 5–8210, 1967.

Perrow, C. "Departmental Power and Perspectives in Industrial Firms." In M.N. Zald (ed.), *Power in Organizations.* 59–89. Nashville: Vanderbilt University Press, 1970.

Perry, R.B. *Realms of Value.* Cambridge, MA: Harvard University Press, 1954.

Peters, T. and Austin, N. *A Passion for Excellence.* New York: Random House, 1985.

Peters, T. and Waterman, R. *In Search of Excellence: Lessons from America's Best-Run Companies.* New York: Harper & Row, 1983.

Pettigrew, A.M., "On Studying Organizational Cultures." *Administrative Science Quarterly* 24, no. 4 (1979): 570–81.

Pfeffer, J. "Management as Symbolic Action: The Creation and Maintenance of Organizational Paradigms." In L. Cummings and B. Staw (eds.), *Research in Organizational Behavior,* vol. 3. Greenwich, CT: JAI Press, 1981a.

———. *Power In Organizations.* Marshfield, MA: Pitman Publishing Company, 1981b.

Pfeffer, J. and Leong, A. "Resource Allocations in United Funds: Examination of Power and Dependence." *Social Forces* 55 (1977): 775–90.

Pfeffer, J. and Salancik, G.R. "Organizational Decision Making as a Political Process: The Case of a University Budget." *Administrative Science Quarterly* 19 (1974): 135–51.

———. *The External Control of Organizations: A Resource Dependence Perspective.* New York: Harper & Row, 1978.

Pondy, L. and Mitroff, I. "Beyond Open System Models of Organization." In B. Staw (ed.), *Research in Organizational Behavior,* vol. 1. Greenwich, CT: JAI Press, 1979.

Provan, K.G.; Beyer, J.M.; and Krytbosch, C. "Environmental Linkages and Power in Resource Dependence Relations between Organizations." *Administrative Science Quarterly* 25 (1980): 200–25.

Ranson, S.; Hinings, B.; and Royston, G. "The Structuring of Organizational Structures." *Administrative Science Quarterly* 25 (1980): 1–17.

Rettig, S. and Pasamanick, B. "Changes in Moral Values Among College Students: A Factorial Study." *American Sociological Review* 24 (1959): 856–63.

Rokeach, M. *Beliefs, Attitudes, and Values.* San Francisco: Jossey-Bass Inc., 1968.

———. *The Nature of Human Values.* New York: Free Press, 1973.

Rose, A. "Sociology and the Study of Values." *British Journal of Sociology* 7 (1956): 1–17.

Rosenberg, M. *Occupations and Values.* Glencoe, IL: Free Press, 1957.

Rothschild-Whitt, J. "The Collectivist Organization: An Alternative To Rational-Bureaucratic Models." *American Sociological Review* 44 (1979): 509–27.

Ruch, R.S. and Goodman, R. *Image At The Top.* New York: Free Press, 1983.

Russell, B. *Power: A New Social Analysis.* London: George Allen & Unwin, 1938.

Salancik, G.R. and Pfeffer, J. "The Bases and Use of Power in Organizational Decision Making: The Case of a University." *Administrative Science Quarterly* 19 (1974): 453–73.

————. "Who Gets Power—And How They Hold On to It: A Strategic Contingencies Model of Power." *Organizational Dynamics* 5 (1977): 3–21.

Salancik, G.R.; Pfeffer, J.; and Kelly, J.P. "A Contingency Model of Influence in Organizational Decision-Making." *Pacific Sociological Review* 21 (1978): 239–56.

Sathe, V. "Implications of Corporate Culture: A Manager's Guide to Action." *Organizational Dynamics* 9 (1983): 333–54.

————. "How to Decipher and Change Corporate Culture." In R.H. Kilmann, M.J. Saxton, R. Serpa, and associates (eds.). *Gaining Control of the Corporate Culture,* 230–61. San Francisco: Jossey-Bass Inc., 1985.

Satow, R.L. "Value-Rational Authority and Professional Organizations: Weber's Missing Type." *Administrative Science Quarterly* 20 (1975): 526–31.

Saunders, C.S. and Scamell, R. "Intraorganizational Distribution of Power: Replication Research." *Academy of Management Journal* 25, no. 1 (1982): 192–200.

Scheff, T.J. "Toward A Sociological Model of Consensus." *American Sociological Review* 32, no. 1 (1967): 32–54.

Schein, E.H. "The Role of the Founder in Creating Organizational Culture." *Organizational Dynamics* (Summer 1983): 13–28.

————. "Organizational Socialization and the Profession of Management." *Industrial Management Review* 9 (1968): 1–6.

————. *Organizational Culture and Leadership.* San Francisco: Jossey-Bass, 1985.

Schmidt, W.H. and Posner, B.Z. *Managerial Values and Expectations: The Silent Power in Personal and Organizational Life.* New York: American Management Association, 1982.

————. *Managerial Values in Perspective.* New York: American Management Association, 1983.

Schopler, J. "Social Power." In L. Berkowitz (ed.) *Advances in Experimental Social Psychology,* vol. 2, 177–218. New York: Academic Press, 1965.

Schwartz, H., and Davis, S. M., "Matching Corporate Culture and Business Strategy." *Organizational Dynamics* 10 (Summer 1981): 30–48.

Scott, W. *Values and Organizations: A Study of Fraternities and Sororities.* Chicago: Rand McNally, 1965.

Selznick, P. *Leadership in Administration: A Sociological Interpretation.* Evanston, IL: Row, Peterson & Co., 1957.

Senger, J. "Managers' Perceptions of Subordinates' Competence as a Function of Personal Value Orientations." *Academy of Management Journal* 14 (1971): 415–23.

Shaw, M.E. *Group Dynamics: The Psychology of Small Group Behavior.* 3d ed. New York: McGraw-Hill, 1981.

Shorr, J. "The Development of a Test to Measure the Intensity of Values." *Journal of Educational Psychology* 44 (1953): 266–74.

Short, L.E. and Farratt, T.W. "Work Unit Culture: Strategic Starting Point in Building Organizational Change." *Management Review* 23 (August 1984): 15–19.

Silverzweig, S. and Allen, R.F. "Changing the Corporate Culture." *Sloan Management Review* 17 (Spring 1976): 33–49.

Smith, A. *The Wealth of Nations.* Middlesex, England: Penguin (1970). [first published, 1776.]

Smircich, L. "Studying Organizations as Cultures." In G. Morgan, *Beyond Method,* 160–74. Beverly Hills: Sage Publishing, 1983a.

———. "Concepts of Culture and Organizational Analysis." *Administrative Science Quarterly* 28, no. 3 (1983b): 339–59.

Snow, C.C. and Hambrick, D.C. "Measuring Organizational Strategies: Some Theoretical and Methodological Problems." *The Academy of Management Review* 5, no. 4 (1980): 527–38.

Sproull, L.S. "Beliefs in Organizations." In Paul C. Nystrom and William H. Starbuck (eds.) *Handbook of Organizational Design,* vol. 2, 203–24. New York: Oxford University Press, 1981.

Starbuck, W.H. "Congealing Oil: Inventing Ideologies to Justify Acting Ideologies Out." *Journal of Management Studies* 19, no. 1 (1982): 3–27.

Steers, R.M. *Organizational Effectiveness: A Behavioral View.* Santa Monica, CA: Goodyear, 1977.

Stinchcombe, A.L. *Constructing Social Theories.* New York: Harcourt, Brace & World, 1968.

Tagiuri, R. "Value Orientations and the Relationship of Managers and Scientists." *Administrative Science Quarterly* 10 (1965): 39–51.

Tannenbaum, A.S. *Control in Organizations.* New York: McGraw-Hill, 1968.

Tannenbaum, A.S. and Kahn, R.L. *Participation in Union Locals.* New York: Harper & Row, 1958.

Thompson, J.D. *Organizations in Action.* New York: McGraw-Hill, 1967.

Tichy, N.M. "Managing Change Strategically: The Technical, Political, and Cultural Keys." *Organizational Dynamics* 11 (Autumn 1982): 59–80.

Van Maanen, J. and Schein, E.H. "Toward A Theory of Organizational Socialization." In B. Staw (ed.), *Research in Organizational Behavior,* vol. 1, 209–264. Greenwich, CT: JAI Press, 1979.

Watson, J.G. and Simpson, L.R. "A Comparative Study of Owner-Manager Personnel Values in Black and White Small Businesses." *Academy of Management Journal* 21 (1978): 313–19.

Weber, M. *The Theory of Social and Economic Organization.* Translated by A.M. Henderson and T. Parsons. New York: The Free Press, 1947.

———. *Economy and Society,* vol. 2. Berkeley, CA: University of California Press, 1968.

Weick, K.E. *The Social Psychology of Organizing.* Reading, Mass: Addison-Wesley, 1969.

Weiss, A. and Enz, C.A. *A Conceptual Note on the Relationship among Power, Politics, and Authority.* Unpublished manuscript, 1985.

Weiss, H.M. "Social Learning of Work Values in Organizations." *Journal of Applied Psychology* 63 (1978): 711–18.

Wilkins, A.L. "The Culture Audit: A Tool for Understanding Organizations." *Organizational Dynamics* 12 (Autumn 1983): 24–38.

———. "Organizational Stories as Symbols which Control the Organization." In L. Pondy, P. Frost, G. Morgan, and T. Dandridge, *Organizational Behavior and Industrial Relations* (Monographs in *Organizational Symbolism,* vol. 1), 81–92. Greenwich, CT: JAI Press, 1983.

Williams, R.M. *American Society: A Sociological Interpretation.* New York: Knopf, 1960.

Withey, S. "The U.S. and the U.S.S.R.: A Report of the Public's Perspective on United States-Russian Relations in Late 1961." In D. Bobrow (ed.), *Components of Defense Policy,* 164–74. Chicago: Rand McNally, 1965.

Wollack, S., Goodale, J.; Wijting, J.; and Smith, P. "Development of the Survey of Work Values." *Journal of Applied Psychology* 55, no. 4 (1971): 331–38.

Woodruff, A.D. "Personal Values and the Direction of Behavior." *School Review* 50 (1942): 32–42.

Wrong, D.H. "The Oversocialized Conception of Man in Modern Sociology." *American Sociological Review* 26 (1961): 183–93.

———. "Some Problems in Defining Social Power." *The American Journal of Sociology* 23 (1968): 673–81.

———. *Power: Its Forms, Bases, and Uses.* New York: Harper Colophon Books, 1979.

Zenzen, M.J. and Hammer, L.Z. "Value Measurement and Existential Wholeness: A Critique of the Rokeachean Approach to Value Research." *The Journal of Value Inquiry* 14 (1980): 142–56.

Zimmerman, D.H. and Pollner, M. "The Everyday World as a Phenomenon." In J. Douglas (ed.), *Understanding Everyday Life* 33–65. Chicago: Aldine, 1970.

Zucker, L.G., "The Role of Institutionalization in Cultural Persistence." *American Sociological Review* 42 (1977): 726–43.

Index